The Gracchi, Mariu
By A.H. Beesley

PREFACE

It would be scarcely possible for anyone writing on the period embraced in this volume, to perform his task adequately without making himself familiar with Mr. Long's 'History of the Decline of the Roman Republic' and Mommsen's 'History of Rome.' To do over again (as though the work had never been attempted) what has been done once for all accurately and well, would be mere prudery of punctiliousness. But while I acknowledge my debt of gratitude to both these eminent historians, I must add that for the whole period I have carefully examined the original authorities, often coming to conclusions widely differing from those of Mr. Long. And I venture to hope that from the advantage I have had in being able to compare the works of two writers, one of whom has well-nigh exhausted the theories as the other has the facts of the subject, I have succeeded in giving a more consistent and faithful account of the leaders and legislation of the revolutionary era than has hitherto been written. Certainly there could be no more instructive commentary on either history than the study of the other, for each supplements the other and emphasizes its defects. If Mommsen at times pushes conjecture to the verge of invention, as in his account of the junction of the Helvetii and Cimbri, Mr. Long, in his dogged determination never to swerve from facts to inference, falls into the opposite extreme, resorting to somewhat Cyclopean architecture in his detestation of stucco. But my admiration for his history is but slightly qualified by such considerations, and to any student who may be stimulated by the volumes of this series to acquire what would virtually amount to an acquaintance first-hand with the narratives of ancient writers, I would say 'Read Mr. Long's history.' To do so is to learn not only knowledge but a lesson in historical study generally. For the writings of a man with whom style is not the first object are as refreshing as his scorn for romancing history is wholesome, and the grave irony with which he records its slips amusing.

A.H.B.

CHAPTER I.ANTECEDENTS OF THE REVOLUTION.

During the last half of the second century before Christ Rome was undisputed mistress of the civilised world. A brilliant period of foreign conquest had succeeded the 300 years in which she had overcome her neighbours and made herself supreme in Italy. In 146 B.C. she had given the death-blow to her greatest rival, Carthage, and had annexed Greece. In 140 treachery had rid her of Viriathus, the stubborn guerilla who defied her generals and defeated her armies in Spain. In 133 the terrible fate of Numantia, and in 132 the merciless suppression of the Sicilian slave-revolt, warned all foes of the Republic that the sword, which the incompetence of many generals had made seem duller than of old, was still keen to smite; and except where some slave-bands were in desperate rebellion, and in Pergamus, where a pretender disputed with Rome the legacy of Attalus, every land along the shores of the Mediterranean was subject to or at the mercy of a town not half as large as the London of to-day. Almost exactly a century afterwards the Government under which this gigantic empire had been consolidated was no more.

Foreign wars will have but secondary importance in the following pages. [The history will not be one of military events.] The interest of the narrative centres mainly in home politics; and though the world did not cease to echo to the tramp of conquering legions, and the victorious soldier became a more and more important factor in the State, still military matters no longer, as in the Samnite and Punic wars, absorb the attention, dwarfed as they are by the great social struggle of which the metropolis was the arena. In treating of the first half of those hundred years of revolution, which began with the tribunate of Tiberius Gracchus and ended with the battle of Actium, it is mainly the fall of the Republican and the foreshadowing of the Imperial system of government which have to be described. [In order to understand the times of the Gracchi it is necessary to understand the history of the orders at Rome.] But, in order to understand rightly the events of those fifty years, some survey, however brief, of the previous history of the Roman orders is indispensable.

When the mists of legend clear away we see a community which, if we do not take slaves into account, consisted of two parts—the governing body, or patres, to whom alone the term Populus Romanus strictly applied, and who constituted the Roman State, and the governed class, or clientes, who were outside its pale. The word patrician, more familiar to our ear than the substantive from which it is formed, came to imply much more than its original meaning. In its simplest and earliest sense it was applied to a man who was sprung from a Roman marriage, who stood towards his client on much the same footing which, in the mildest form of slavery, a master occupies towards his slave. As the patronus was to the libertus, when it became customary to liberate slaves, so in some measure were the Fathers to their retainers, the Clients. That the community was originally divided into these two sections is known. What is not known is how, besides this primary division of patres and clientes, there arose a second political class in the State, namely the plebs. The client as client had no political existence. [The plebeians.] But as a plebeian he had. Whether the plebs was formed of clients who had been released from their clientship, just as slaves might be manumitted; or of foreigners, as soldiers, traders, or artisans were admitted into the community; or partly of foreigners and partly of clients, the latter being equalised by the patres with the former in self-defence; and whether as a name it dated from or was antecedent to the so-called Tullian organization is uncertain. But we know that in one way or other a second political division in the State arose and that the constitution, of which Servius Tullius was the reputed author, made every freeman in Rome a citizen by giving him a vote in the Comitia Centuriata. Yet though the plebeian was a citizen, and as such acquired 'commercium,' or the right to hold and devise property, it was only after a prolonged struggle that he achieved political equality with the patres. [Gradual acquisition by the plebs of political equality with the patres.] Step by step he wrung from them the rights of intermarriage and of filling offices of state; and the great engine by which this was brought about was the tribunate, the historical importance of which dates from, even though as a plebeian magistracy it may have existed before, the first secession of the plebs in 494 B.C. The tribunate stood towards the freedom of the Roman people in something of the same relation which the press of our time occupies towards modern liberty: for its existence implied free criticism of the executive, and out of free speech grew free action. [The Roman government transformed from oligarchy into a plutocracy.]

Side by side with those external events which made Rome mistress first of her neighbours, then, of Italy, and lastly of the world, there went on a succession of internal changes, which first transformed a pure oligarchy into a plutocracy, and secondly overthrew this modified form of oligarchy, and substituted Caesarism. With the earlier of these changes we are concerned here but little. The political revolution was over when the social revolution which we have to record began. But the roots of the social revolution were of deep growth, and were in fact sometimes identical with those of the political revolution.

Englishmen can understand such an intermixture the more readily from the analogies, more or less close, which their own history supplies. They have had a monarchy. They have been ruled by an oligarchy, which has first confronted and then coalesced with the moneyed class, and the united orders have been forced to yield theoretical equality to almost the entire nation, while still retaining real authority in their own hands. They have seen a middle class coquetting with a lower class in order to force an upper class to share with it its privileges, and an upper class resorting in its turn to the same alliance; and they may have noted something more than a superficial resemblance between the tactics of the patres and nobiles of Rome and our own magnates of birth and commerce. Even now they are witnessing the displacement of political by social questions, and, it is to be hoped, the successful solution of problems which in the earlier stages of society have defied the efforts of every statesman. Yet they know that, underlying all the political struggles of their history, questions connected with the rights and interests of rich and poor, capitalist and toiler, land-owner and land-cultivator, have always been silently and sometimes violently agitated. Political emancipation has enabled social discontent to organize itself and find permanent utterance, and we are to-day facing some of the demands to satisfy which the Gracchi sacrificed their lives more than 2,000 years ago. us indeed the wages question is of more prominence than the land question, because we are a manufacturing nation; but the principles at stake are much the same. At Rome social agitation was generally agrarian, and the first thing necessary towards understanding the Gracchan revolution is to gain a clear conception of the history of the public land.

The ground round a town like Rome was originally cultivated by the inhabitants, some of whom, as more food and clothing were required, would settle on the soil. From them the ranks of the army were recruited; and, thus doubly oppressed by military service and by the land tax, which had to be paid in coin, the small husbandman was forced to borrow from some richer man in the town. Hence arose usury, and a class of debtors; and the sum of debt must have been increased as well as the number of the debtors by the very means adopted to relieve it. When Rome conquered a town she confiscated a portion of its territory, and disposed of it in one of four ways. 1. After expelling the owners, she sent some of her own citizens to settle upon it. They did not cease to be Romans, and, being in historical times taken almost exclusively from the plebs, must often have been but poorly furnished with the capital necessary for cultivating the ground. 2. She sold it; and, as with us, when a field is sold, a plan is made of its dimensions and boundaries, so plans of the land thus sold were made on tablets of bronze, and kept by the State. 3. She allowed private persons to 'occupy' it on payment of 'vectigal,' or a portion of the produce; and, though not surrendering the title to the land, permitted the possessors to use it as their private property for purchase, sale, and succession. [Commons.] 4. A portion was kept as common pasture land for those to whom the land had been given or sold, or by whom it was occupied and those who used it paid 'scriptura,' or a tax of so much per head on the beasts, for whose grazing they sent in a return. This irregular system was fruitful in evil. It suited the patres with whom it originated, for they were for a time the sole gainers by it. Without money it must have been hopeless to occupy tracts distant from Rome. The poor man who did so would either involve himself in debt, or be at the mercy of his richer neighbours, whose flocks would overrun his fields, or who might oust him altogether from them by force, and even seize him himself and enroll him as a slave. The rich man, on the other hand, could use such land for pasture, and leave the care of his flocks and herds to clients and slaves. [This irregular system the germ of latifundia.] So originated those 'latifundia,' or large farms, which greatly contributed to the ruin of Rome and Italy. The tilled land grew less and with it dwindled the free population and the recruiting field for the army. Gangs of slaves became more numerous, and were treated with increased brutality; and as men who do not work for their own money are more profuse in spending it than those who do, the extravagance of the Roman possessors helped to swell the tide of luxury, which rose steadily with foreign conquest, and to create in the capital a class free in name indeed, but more degraded, if less miserable, than the very slaves, who were treated like beasts through Italy. It is not certain whether anyone except a patrician could claim 'occupation' as a right; but, as the possessors could in any case sell the land to plebeians, it fell into the hands of rich men, to whichever class they belonged, both at Rome, and in the Roman colonies, and the Municipia; and as it was never really their property—'dominium'—but the property of the State, it was a constant source of envy and discontent among the poor.

[Why complaints about the Public Land became louder at the close of the second century B.C.] As long as fresh assignations of land and the plantations of colonies went on, this discontent could be kept within bounds. But for a quarter of a century preceding our period scarcely any fresh acquisitions of land had been made in Italy, and, with no hope of new allotments from the territory of their neighbours, the people began to clamour for the restitution of their own. [Previous agrarian legislation. Spurius Cassius.] The first attempt to wrest public land from possessors had been made long before this by Spurius Cassius; and he had paid for his daring with his life. [The Licinian Law.] More than a century later the Licinian law forbade anyone to hold above 500 'jugera' of public land, for which, moreover, a tenth of the arable and a fifth of the grazing produce was to be paid to the State. The framers of the law are said to have hoped that possessors of more than this amount would shrink from making on oath a false return of the land which they occupied, and that, as they would be liable to penalties for exceeding the prescribed maximum, all land beyond the maximum would be sold at a nominal price (if this interpretation of the [Greek: kat' oligon] of Appian may be hazarded) to the poor. It is probable that they did not quite know what they were aiming at, and certain that they did not foresee the effects of their measure. In a confused way the law may have been meant to comprise sumptuary, political, and agrarian objects. It forbade anyone to keep more than a hundred large or five hundred small beasts on the common pasture-land, and stipulated for the employment of a certain proportion of free labour. The free labourers were to give information of the crops produced, so that the fifths and tenths might be duly paid; and it may have been the breakdown of such an impossible institution which led to the establishment of the 'publicani.' [Composite nature of the Licinian law.] Nothing, indeed, is more likely than that Licinius and Sextius should have attempted to remedy by one measure the specific grievance of the poor plebeians, the political disabilities of the rich plebeians and the general deterioration of public morals; but, though their motives may have been patriotic, such a measure could no more cure the body politic than a man who has a broken limb, is blind, and in a consumption can be made sound at every point by the heal-all of a quack. Accordingly the Licinian law was soon, except in its political provisions, a dead letter. Licinius was the first man prosecuted for its violation, and the economical desire of the nation became intensified. [The Flaminian law.] In 232 B.C. Flaminius carried a law for the distribution of land taken from the Senones among the plebs. Though the law turned out no possessors, it was opposed by the Senate and nobles. Nor is this surprising, for any law distributing land was both actually and as a precedent a blow to the interests of the class which practised occupation. What is at first sight surprising is that small parcels of land, such as must have been assigned in these distributions, should have been so coveted. [Why small portions of land were so coveted.] The explanation is probably fourfold. Those who clamoured for them were wretched enough to clutch at any change; or did not realise to themselves the dangers and drawbacks of what they desired; or intended at once to sell their land to some richer neighbour; or, lastly, longed to keep a slave or two, just as the primary object of the 'mean white' in America used to be to keep his negro. [Failure of previous legislation.] On the whole, it is clear that legislation previous to this period had not diminished agrarian grievances, and it is clear also why these grievances were so sorely felt. The general tendency at Rome and throughout Italy was towards a division of society into two classes—the very rich and the very poor, a tendency which increased so fast that not many years later it was said that out of some 400,000 men at Rome only 2,000 could, in spite of the city being notoriously the centre to which the world's wealth gravitated, be called really rich men. To any patriot the progressive extinction of small land-owners must have seemed piteous in itself and menacing to the life of the State. On the other hand, the poor had always one glaring act of robbery to cast in the teeth of the rich. A sanguine tribune might hope permanently to check a growing evil by fresh supplies of free labour. His poor partisan again had a direct pecuniary interest in getting the land. Selfish and philanthropic motives therefore went hand in hand, and in advocating the distribution of land a statesman would be sure of enlisting the sympathies of needy Italians, even more than those of the better-provided-for poor of Rome.

[Roman slavery.] Incidental mention has been made of the condition of the slaves in Italy. It was the sight of the slave-gangs which partly at least roused Tiberius Gracchus to action, and some remarks on Roman slavery follow naturally an enquiry into the nature of the public land. The most terrible characteristic of slavery is that it blights not only the unhappy slaves themselves, but their owners and the land where they live. It is an absolutely unmitigated evil. As Roman conquests multiplied and luxury increased, enormous fortunes became more common, and the demand for slaves increased also. Ten thousand are said to have been landed and sold at Delos in one day. What proportion the slave population of Italy bore to the free at the time of the Gracchi we cannot say. It has been placed as low as 4 per cent., but the probability is that it was far greater. [Slave labour universally employed.] In trades, mining, grazing, levying of revenue, and every field of speculation, slave-labour was universally employed. If it is certain that even unenfranchised Italians, however poor, could be made to serve in the Roman army, it was a proprietor's direct interest from that point of view to employ slaves, of whose services he could not be deprived.

[Whence the slaves came. Their treatment.] A vast impetus had been given to the slave-trade at the time of the conquest of Macedonia, about thirty-five years before our period. The great slave-producing countries were those bordering on the Mediterranean—Africa, Asia, Spain, &c. An organized system of man-hunting supplied the Roman markets, and slave-dealers were part of the ordinary retinue of a Roman army. When a batch of slaves reached its destination they were kept in a pen till bought. Those bought for domestic service would no doubt be best off, and the cunning, mischievous rogue, the ally of the young against the old master of whom we read in Roman comedy, if he does not come up to our ideal of what a man should be, does not seem to have been physically very wretched. Even here, however, we see how degraded a thing a slave was, and the frequent threats of torture prove how utterly he was at the mercy of a cruel master's caprice. We know, too, that when a master was arraigned on a criminal charge, the first thing done to prove his guilt was to torture his slaves. But just as in America the popular figure of the oily, lazy, jocular negro, brimming over with grotesque good-humour and screening himself in the weakness of an indulgent master, merely served to brighten a picture of which the horrible plantation system was the dark background; so at Rome no instances of individual indulgence were a set-off against the monstrous barbarities which in the end brought about their own punishment, and the ruin of the Republic. [Dread inspired by the prospect of Roman slavery.] Frequent stories attest the horrors of Roman slavery felt by conquered nations. We read often of individuals, and sometimes of whole towns, committing suicide sooner than fall into the conquerors' hands. Sometimes slaves slew their dealers, sometimes one another. A boy in Spain killed his three sisters and starved himself to avoid slavery. Women killed their children with the same object. If, as it is asserted, the plantation-system was not yet introduced into Italy, such stories, and the desperate out-breaks, and almost incredibly merciless suppression of slave revolts, prove that the condition of the Roman slave was sufficiently miserable. [The horrors of slavery culminated in Sicily.] But doubtless misery reached its climax in Sicily, where that system was in full swing. Slaves not sold for domestic service were there branded and often made to work in chains, the strongest serving as shepherds. Badly fed and clothed, these shepherds plundered whenever they found the chance. Such brigandage was winked at, and sometimes positively encouraged, by the owners, while the governors shrank from punishing the brigands for fear of offending their masters. As the demand for slaves grew, slave-breeding as well as slave-importation was practised. No doubt there were as various theories as to the most profitable management of slaves then as in America lately. Damophilus had the instincts of a Legree: a Haley and a Cato would have held much the same sentiments as to the rearing of infants. Some masters would breed and rear, and try to get more work from the slave by kindness than harshness. Others would work them off and buy afresh; and as this would be probably the cheapest policy, no doubt it was the prevalent one. And what an appalling vista of dumb suffering do such considerations open to us! Cold, hunger, nakedness, torture, infamy, a foreign country, a strange climate, a life so hard that it made the early death which was almost inevitable a comparative blessing—such was the terrible lot of the Roman slave. At last, almost simultaneously at various places in the Roman dominions, he turned like a beast upon a brutal drover. [Outbreaks in various quarters.] At Rome, at Minturnae, at Sinuessa, at Delos, in Macedonia, and in Sicily insurrections or attempts at insurrections broke out. They were everywhere mercilessly suppressed, and by wholesale torture and crucifixion the conquerors tried to clothe death, their last ally, with terror which even a slave dared not encounter. In the year when Tiberius Gracchus was tribune (and the coincidence is significant), it was found necessary to send a consul to put down the first slave revolt in Sicily. It is not known when it broke out. [Story of Damophilus.] Its proximate cause was the brutality of Damophilus, of Enna, and his wife Megallis. His slaves consulted a man named Eunous, a Syrian-Greek, who had long foretold that he would be a king, and whom his master's guests had been in the habit of jestingly asking to remember them when he came to the throne. [The first Sicilian slave war.] Eunous led a band of 400 against Enna. He could spout fire from his mouth, and his juggling and prophesying inspired confidence in his followers. All the men of Enna were slain except the armourers, who were fettered and compelled to forge arms. Damophilus and Megallis were brought with every insult into the theatre. He began to beg for his life with some effect, but Hermeias and another cut him down; and his wife, after being tortured by the women, was cast over a precipice. But their daughter had been gentle to the slaves, and they not only did not harm her, but sent her under an escort, of which this Hermeias was one, to Catana. Eunous was now made king, and called himself Antiochus. He made Achaeus his general, was joined by Cleon with 5,000 slaves, and soon mustered 10,000 men. Four praetors (according to Florus) were defeated; the number of the rebels rapidly increased to 200,000; and the whole island except a few towns was at their mercy. In 134 the consul Flaccus went to Sicily; but with what result is not known. In 133 the consul L. Calpurnius Piso captured Messana, killed 8,000 slaves, and crucified all his prisoners. In 132 P. Rupilius captured the two strongholds of the slaves, Tauromenium and Enna (Taormina and Castragiovanni). Both towns stood on the top ledges of precipices, and were hardly accessible. Each was blockaded and each was eventually surrendered by a traitor. But at Tauromenium the defenders held out, it is said, till all food was gone, and they had eaten the children, and the women, and some of the men. Cleon's brother Comanus was taken here; all the prisoners were first tortured, and then thrown down the rocks. At Enna Cleon made a gallant sally, and died of his wounds. Eunous fled and was pulled out of a pit with his cook, his baker, his bathman, and his fool. He is said to have died in prison of the same disease as Sulla and Herod. Rupilius crucified over 20,000 slaves, and so quenched with blood the last fires of rebellion.

Besides the dangers threatening society from the discontent of the poor, the aggressions of the rich, the multiplication and ferocious treatment of slaves, and the social rivalries of the capital, the condition of Italy and the general deterioration of public morality imperatively demanded reform. It has been already said that we do not know for certain how the plebs arose. But we know how it wrested political equality from the patres, and, speaking roughly, we may date the fusion of the two orders under he common title 'nobiles,' from the Licinian laws. [The 'nobiles' at Rome.] It had been a gradual change, peaceably brought about, and the larger number having absorbed the smaller, the term 'nobiles,' which specifically meant those who had themselves filled a curule office, or whose fathers had done so, comprehended in common usage the old nobility and the new. The new nobles rapidly drew aloof from the residuum of the plebs, and, in the true parvenu spirit, aped and outdid the arrogance of the old patricians. Down to the time of the Gracchi, or thereabouts, the two great State parties consisted of the plebs on the one hand, and these nobles on the other. [The 'optimates' and 'populares.'] After that date new names come into use, though we can no more fix the exact time when the terms optimates and populares superseded previous party watchwords than we can when Tory gave place to Conservative, and Whig to Liberal. Thus patricians and plebeians were obsolete terms, and nobles and plebeians no longer had any political meaning, for each was equal in the sight of the law; each had a vote; each was eligible to every office. But when the fall of Carthage freed Rome from all rivals, and conquest after conquest filled the treasury, increased luxury made the means of ostentation more greedily sought. Office meant plunder; and to gain office men bribed, and bribed every day on a vaster scale. If we said that 'optimates' signified the men who bribed and abused office under the banner of the Senate and its connections, and that 'populares' meant men who bribed and abused office with the interests of the people outside the senatorial pale upon their lips, we might do injustice to many good men on both sides, but should hardly be slandering the parties. Parties in fact they were not. They were factions, and the fact that it is by no means easy always to decide how far individuals were swayed by good or bad motives, where good motives were so often paraded to mask base actions, does not disguise their despicable character. Honest optimates would wish to maintain the Senate's preponderance from affection to it, and from belief in its being the mainstay of the State. Honest populares, like the Gracchi, who saw the evils of senatorial rule, tried to win the popular vote to compass its overthrow. Dishonest politicians of either side advocated conservatism or change simply from the most selfish personal ambition; and in time of general moral laxity it is the dishonest politicians who give the tone to a party. The most unscrupulous members of the ruling ring, the most shameless panderers to mob prejudice, carry all before them. Both seek one thing only—personal ascendency, and the State becomes the bone over which the vilest curs wrangle.

[Who the equites were.] In writing of the Gracchi reference will be made to the Equites. The name had broadened from its original meaning, and now merely denoted all non-senatorial rich men. An individual eques would lean to the senatorial faction or the faction of men too poor to keep a horse for cavalry service, just as his connexions were chiefly with the one or the other. How, as a body, the equites veered round alternately to each side, we shall see hereafter. Instead of forming a sound middle class to check the excesses of both parties, they were swayed chiefly by sordid motives, and backed up the men who for the time seemed most willing or able to gratify their greed. What went on at Rome must have been repeated over again with more or less exactitude throughout Italy, and there, in addition to this process of national disintegration, the clouds of a political storm were gathering. The following table will show at a glance the classification of the Roman State as constituted at the outbreak of the Social War.

Cives Romani: 1. Rome 2. Roman Colonies 3. Municipia
Roman Colonies and Municipia are Praefectura.
  Peregrini:
  1. Latini or Nomen Latinum
     a. Old Latin towns except such as had been made Municipia
     b. Colonies of old Latin towns
     c. Joint colonies (if any) of Rome and old Latin towns
     d. Colonies of Italians from all parts of Italy founded by Rome
        under the name of Latin Colonies
  2. Socii, i.e. Free inhabitants of Italy
  3. Provincials, i.e. Free subjects of Rome out of Italy

[Rights of Cives Romani.] The Cives Romani in and out of Rome had the Jus Suffragii and the Jus Honorum, i.e. the right to vote and the right to hold office. [The Roman Colony.] A Roman Colony was in its organization Rome in miniature, and the people among whom it had been planted as a garrison may either have retained their own political constitution, or have been governed by a magistrate sent from Rome. They were not Roman citizens except as being residents of a Roman city, but by irregular marriages with Romans the line of demarcation between the two peoples may have grown less clearly defined. [The Praefectura.] Praefectura was the generic name for Roman colonies and for all Municipia to which prefects were sent annually to administer justice. [Municipia] Municipia are supposed to have been originally those conquered Italian towns to which Connubium and Commercium, i.e. rights of intermarriage and of trade, were given, but from whom Jus Suffragii and Jus Honorum were withheld. These privileges, however, were conferred on them before the Social War. Some were governed by Roman magistrates and some were self-governed. They voted in the Roman tribes, though probably only at important crises, such as the agitation for an agrarian law. They were under the jurisdiction of the Praetor Urbanus, but vicarious justice was administered among them by an official called Praefectus juri dicundo, sent yearly from Rome.

[The Latini.] The Latini had no vote at Rome, no right of holding offices, and were practically Roman subjects. A Roman who joined a Latin colony ceased to be a Roman citizen. Whether there was any difference between the internal administration of a Latin colony and an old Latin town is uncertain. The Latini may have had Commercium and Connubium, or only the former. They certainly had not Jus Suffragii or Jus Honorum, and they were in subjection to Rome. A Latin could obtain the Roman franchise, but the mode of doing so at this time is a disputed point. Livy mentions a law which enabled a Latin to obtain the franchise by migrating to Rome and being enrolled in the census, provided he left children behind him to fill his place. There is no doubt that either legally or irregularly Latini did migrate to Rome and did so obtain the citizenship, but we know no more. Others say that the later right by which a Latin obtained the citizenship in virtue of filling a magistracy in his native town existed already.

[The Socii.] Of the Socii, all or many of them had treaties defining their relations to Rome, and were therefore known as Foederatae Civitates. They had internal self-government, but were bound to supply Rome with soldiers, ships, and sailors.

[Grievances of the Latins and allies.] At the time of the Gracchi discontent was seething among the Latins and allies. There were two classes among them—the rich landlords and capitalists, who prospered as the rich at Rome prospered, and the poor who were weighed down by debt or were pushed out of their farms by slave-labour, or were hangers-on of the rich in the towns and eager for distributions of land. The poor were oppressed no doubt by the rich men both of their own cities and of Rome. The rich chafed at the intolerable insolence of Roman officials. It was not that Rome interfered with the local self-government she had granted by treaty, but the Italians laboured under grievous disabilities and oppression. So late as the Jugurthine war, Latin officers were executed by martial law, whereas any Roman soldier could appeal to a civil tribunal. Again, while the armies had formerly been recruited from the Romans and the allies equally, now the severest service and the main weight of wars fell on the latter, who furnished, moreover, two soldiers to every Roman. Again, without a certain amount of property, a man at Rome could not be enrolled in the army; but the rule seems not to have applied to Italians. Nor was the civil less harsh than the military administration. A consul's wife wished to use the men's bath at Teanum; and because the bathers were not cleared out quickly enough, and the baths were not clean enough, M. Marius, the chief magistrate of the town, was stripped and scourged in the market-place. A free herdsman asked in joke if it was a corpse that was in a litter passing through Venusia, and which contained a young Roman. Though not even an official, its occupant showed that, if lazy, he was at least alive, by having the peasant whipped to death with the litter straps. In short, the rich Italians would feel the need of the franchise as strongly as the old plebeians had felt it, and all the more strongly because the Romans had not only ceased to enfranchise whole communities, but were chary of giving the citizenship even to individuals. The poor also had the ordinary grievances against their own rich, and were so far likely to favour the schemes of any man who assailed the capitalist class, Roman or Italian, as a whole; but they none the less disliked Roman supremacy, and would be easily persuaded to attribute to that supremacy some of the hardships which it did not cause.

[State of the transmarine provinces.] While such fires were slowly coming to the surface in Italy, and were soon to flame out in the Social War, the state of the provinces out of the peninsula was not more reassuring. The struggle with Viriathus and the Numantine war had revealed the fact that the last place to look for high martial honour or heroic virtue was the Roman army. If a Scipio sustained the traditions of Roman generalship, and a Gracchus those of republican rectitude, other commanders would have stained the military annals of any nation. [Deterioration of Roman generalship.] Roman generals had come to wage war for themselves and not for the State. They even waged it in defiance of the State's express orders. If they found peace in the provinces, they found means to break it, hoping to glut their avarice by pillage or by the receipt of bribes, which it was now quite the exception not to accept, or to win sham laurels and cheap triumphs from some miserable raid on half-armed barbarians. Often these carpet-knights were disgracefully beaten, though infamy in the provinces sometimes became fame at Rome, and then they resorted to shameful trickery repeated again and again. [and of the Army.] The State and the army were worthy of the commanders. The former engaged in perhaps the worst wars that can be waged. Hounded on by its mercantile class, it fought not for a dream of dominion, or to beat back encroaching barbarism, but to exterminate a commercial rival. The latter, which it was hard to recruit on account of the growing effeminacy of the city, it was harder still to keep under discipline. It was followed by trains of cooks, and actors, and the viler appendages of oriental luxury, and was learning to be satisfied with such victories as were won by the assassination of hostile generals, or ratified by the massacre of men who had been guaranteed their lives. The Roman fleet was even more inefficient than the army; and pirates roved at will over the Mediterranean, pillaging this island, waging open war with that, and carrying off the population as slaves. A new empire was rising in the East, as Rome permitted the Parthians to wrest Persia, Babylonia, and Media from the Syrian kings. The selfish maxim, Divide et impera, assumed its meanest form as it was now pursued. It is a poor and cowardly policy for a great nation to pit against each other its semi-civilised dependencies, and to fan their jealousies in order to prevent any common action on their part, or to avoid drawing the sword for their suppression. Slave revolts, constant petty wars, and piracy were preying on the unhappy provincials, and in the Roman protectorate they found no aid. All their harsh mistress did was to turn loose upon them hordes of money-lenders and tax-farmers ('negotiatores,' and 'publicani'), who cleared off what was left by those stronger creatures of prey, the proconsuls. Thus the misery caused by a meddlesome and nerveless national policy was enhanced by a domestic administration based on turpitude and extortion.

[Universal degeneracy of the Government, and decay of the nation.] Everywhere Rome was failing in her duties as mistress of the civilised world. Her own internal degeneracy was faithfully reflected in the abnegation of her imperial duties. When in any country the small-farmer class is being squeezed off the land; when its labourers are slaves or serfs; when huge tracts are kept waste to minister to pleasure; when the shibboleth of art is on every man's lips, but ideas of true beauty in very few men's souls; when the business-sharper is the greatest man in the city, and lords it even in the law courts; when class-magistrates, bidding for high office, deal out justice according to the rank of the criminal; when exchanges are turned into great gambling-houses, and senators and men of title are the chief gamblers; when, in short, 'corruption is universal, when there is increasing audacity, increasing greed, increasing fraud, increasing impurity, and these are fed by increasing indulgence and ostentation; when a considerable

number of trials in the courts of law bring out the fact that the country in general is now regarded as a prey, upon which any number of vultures, scenting it from afar, may safely light and securely gorge themselves; when the foul tribe is amply replenished by its congeners at home, and foreign invaders find any number of men, bearing good names, ready to assist them in robberies far more cruel and sweeping than those of the footpad or burglar'—when such is the tone of society, and such the idols before which it bends, a nation must be fast going down hill. A more repulsive picture can hardly be imagined. A mob, a moneyed class, and an aristocracy almost equally worthless, hating each other, and hated by the rest of the world; Italians bitterly jealous of Romans, and only in better plight than the provinces beyond the sea; more miserable than either, swarms of slaves beginning to brood over revenge as a solace to their sufferings; the land going out of cultivation; native industry swamped by slave-grown imports; the population decreasing; the army degenerating; wars waged as a speculation, but only against the weak; provinces subjected to organized pillage; in the metropolis childish superstition, whole sale luxury, and monstrous vice. The hour for reform was surely come. Who was to be the man?
* * * * *

CHAPTER II.TIBERIUS GRACCHUS.

General expectation would have pointed to Scipio Aemilianus, the conqueror of Numantia and Carthage, and the foremost man at Rome. He was well-meaning and more than ordinarily able, strict and austere as a general, and as a citizen uniting Greek culture with the old Roman simplicity of life. He was full of scorn of the rabble, and did not scruple to express it. 'Silence,' he cried, when he was hissed for what he said about his brother-in-law's death, 'you step-children of Italy!' and when this enraged them still more, he went on: 'Do you think I shall fear you whom I brought to Italy in fetters now that you are loose?' He showed equal scorn for such pursuits as at Rome at least were associated with effeminacy and vice, and expressed in lively language his dislike of singing and dancing. 'Our children are taught disgraceful tricks. They go to actors' schools with sambucas and psalteries. They learn to sing—a thing which our ancestors considered to be a disgrace to freeborn children. When I was told this I could not believe that men of noble rank allowed their children to be taught such things. But being taken to a dancing school I saw—I did upon my honour—more than fifty boys and girls in the school; and among them one boy, quite a child, about twelve years of age, the son of a man who was at that time a candidate for office. And what I saw made me pity the Commonwealth. I saw the child dancing to the castanets, and it was a dance which one of our wretched, shameless slaves would not have danced.' On another occasion he showed a power of quick retort. As censor he had degraded a man named Asellus, whom Mummius afterwards restored to the equites. Asellus impeached Scipio, and taunted him with the unluckiness of his censorship—its mortality, &c. 'No wonder,' said Scipio, 'for the man who inaugurated it rehabilitated you.'

Such anecdotes show that he was a vigorous speaker. He was of a healthy constitution, temperate, brave, and honest in money matters; for he led a simple life, and with all his opportunities for extortion did not die rich. Polybius, the historian, Panaetius, the philosopher, Terence and Lucilius, the poets, and the orator and politician Laelius were his friends. From his position, his talents, and his associations, he seemed marked out as the one man who could and would desire to step forth as the saviour of his country. But such self-sacrifice is not exhibited by men of Scipio's type. Too able to be blind to the signs of the times, they are swayed by instincts too strong for their convictions. An aristocrat of aristocrats, Scipio was a reformer only so far as he thought reform might prolong the reign of his order. From any more radical measures he shrank with dislike, if not with fear. The weak spot often to be found in those cultured aristocrats who coquet with liberalism was fatal to his chance of being a hero. He was a trimmer to the core, who, without intentional dishonesty, stood facing both ways till the hour came when he was forced to range himself on one side or the other, and then he took the side which he must have known to be the wrong one. Palliation of the errors of a man placed in so terribly difficult a position is only just; but laudation of his statesmanship seems absurd. As a statesman he carried not one great measure, and if one was conceived in his circle, he cordially approved of its abandonment. To those who claim for him that he saw the impossibility of those changes which his brother-in-law advocated, it is sufficient to reply that Rome did not rest till those changes had been adopted, and that the hearty co-operation of himself and his friends would have gone far to turn failure into success. But his mind was too narrow to break through the associations which had environed him from his childhood. When Tiberius Gracchus, a nobler man than himself, had suffered martyrdom for the cause with which he had only dallied, he was base enough to quote from Homer [Greek: os apoloito kai allos hotis toiaita ge hoezoi]—'So perish all who do the like again.'

[Tiberius Gracchus.] But the splendid peril which Scipio shrank from encountering, his brother-in-law courted with the fire and passion of youth. Tiberius Sempronius Gracchus was, according to Plutarch, not quite thirty when he was murdered. Plutarch may have been mistaken, and possibly he was thirty-five. His father, whose name he bore, had been a magnificent aristocrat, and his mother was Cornelia, daughter of Hannibal's conqueror, the first Scipio Africanus, and one of the comparatively few women whose names are famous in history. He had much in common with Scipio Aemilianus, whom he resembled in rank and refinement, in valour, in his familiarity with Hellenic culture, and in the style of his speeches. Diophanes, of Mitylene, taught him oratory. The philosopher, Blossius, of Cumae, was his friend. He belonged to the most distinguished circle at Rome. He had married the daughter of Appius, and his brother had married the daughter of Mucianus. He had served under Scipio, and displayed striking bravery at Carthage; and, as quaestor of the incompetent Mancinus, had by his character for probity saved a Roman army from destruction; for the Numantines would not treat with the consul, but only with Gracchus. No man had a more brilliant career open to him at Rome, had he been content only to shut his eyes to the fate that threatened his country. But he had not only insight but a conscience, and cheerfully risked his life to avert the ruin which he foresaw. His character has been as much debated as his measures, and the most opposite conclusions have been formed about both, so that his name is a synonym for patriot with some, for demagogue with others. Even historians of our own day are still at variance as to the nature of his legislation. But from a comparison of their researches, and an independent examination of the authorities on which they are based, something like a clear conception of the plans of Gracchus seems possible. What has never, perhaps, as yet been made sufficiently plain is, who it was that Gracchus especially meant to benefit. Much of the public land previously described lay in the north and south of Italy from the frontier rivers Rubicon and Macra to Apulia. It formed, as Appian says, the largest portion of the land taken from conquered towns by Rome. [Agrarian proposals of Gracchus.] What Gracchus proposed was to take from the rich and give to the poor some of this land. It was, in fact, merely the Licinian law over again with certain modifications, and the existence of that law would make the necessity for a repetition of it inexplicable had it not been a curious principle with the Romans that a law which had fallen into desuetude ceased to be binding. But it actually fell short of the law of Licinius, for it provided that he who surrendered what he held over and above 500 jugera should be guaranteed in the permanent possession of that quantity, and moreover might retain 250 jugera in addition for each of his sons. Some writers conjecture that altogether an occupier might not hold more than 1,000 jugera.

Now the first thing to remark about the law is that it was by no means a demagogue's sop tossed to the city mob which he was courting. Gracchus saw slave labour ruining free labour, and the manhood and soil of Italy and the Roman army proportionately depreciated. [Nothing demagogic about the proposal.] To fill the vacuum he proposed to distribute to the poor not only of Rome but of the Municipia, of the Roman colonies, and, it is to be presumed, of the Socii also, land taken from the rich members of those four component parts of the Roman State. This consideration alone destroys at once the absurd imputation of his being actuated merely by demagogic motives; but in no history is it adequately enforced. No demagogue at that epoch would have spread his nets so wide. At the same time it gives the key to the subsequent manoeuvres by which his enemies strove to divide his partisans. Broadly, then, we may say that Gracchus struck boldly at the very root of the decadence of the whole peninsula, and that if his remedy could not cure it nothing else could. [The Socii—land-owners.] How the Socii became possessors of the public land we do not know. Probably they bought it from Cives Romani, its authorised occupiers, with the connivance of the State. We now see from whom the land was to be taken, namely, the rich all over Italy, and to whom it was to be given, the poor all over Italy; and also the object with which it was to be given, namely, to re-create a peasantry and stop the increase of the slave-plague. [Provision against evasions of the law.] In order to prevent the law becoming a dead letter like that of Licinius, owing to poor men selling their land as soon as they got it, he proposed that the new land-owners should not have the right to dispose of their land to others, and for this, though it would have been hard to carry out, we cannot see what other proviso could have been substituted. Lastly, as death and other causes would constantly render changes in the holdings inevitable, he proposed that a permanent board should have the superintendence of them, and this too was a wise and necessary measure.

[Provision for the administration of the law.] We can understand so much of the law of Gracchus, but it is hard thoroughly to understand more. It has been urged as a difficulty not easily explained that few people, after retaining 500 jugera for themselves and 250 for each of their sons, would have had much left to surrender. But this difficulty is imaginary rather than real; for Appian says that the public land was 'the greater part' of the land taken by Rome from conquered states, and the great families may have had vast tracts of it as pasture land. [Things about the law hard to understand.] There are, however, other things which with our meagre knowledge of the law we cannot explain. For instance, was a hard and fast line drawn at 500 jugera as compensation whether a man surrendered 2 jugera or 2,000 beyond that amount? Again, considering the outcry made, it is hard to imagine that only those possessing above 500 jugera were interfered with. But this perhaps may be accounted for by recollecting that in such matters men fight bravely against what they feel to be the thin end of the wedge, even if they are themselves concerned only sympathetically. What Gracchus meant to do with the slaves displaced by free labour, or how he meant to decide what was public and what was private land after inextricable confusion between the two in many parts for so many years, we cannot even conjecture. The statesmanlike comprehensiveness, however, of his main propositions justifies us in believing that he had not overlooked such obvious stumbling-blocks in his way. [Appian's criticism of the law.] When Appian says he was eager to accomplish what he thought to be a good thing, we concur in the testimony Appian thus gives to Gracchus having been a good man. But when he goes on to say he was so eager that he never even thought of the difficulty, we prefer to judge Gracchus by his own acts rather than by Appian's criticism or the similar criticisms of modern writers. [Speeches of Gracchus explaining his motives.] The speeches ascribed to him, which are apparently genuine, seem to show that he knew well enough what he was about. 'The wild beasts of Italy,' he said, 'have their dens to retire to, but the brave men who spill their blood in her cause have nothing left but air and light. Without homes, without settled habitations, they wander from place to place with their wives and children; and their generals do but mock them when at the head of their armies they exhort their men to fight for their sepulchres and the gods of their hearths, for among such numbers perhaps there is not one Roman who has an altar that has belonged to his ancestors or a sepulchre in which their ashes rest. The private soldiers fight and die to advance the wealth and luxury of the great, and they are called masters of the world without having a sod to call their own.' Again, he asked, 'Is it not just that what belongs to the people should be shared by the people? Is a man with no capacity for fighting more useful to his country than a soldier? Is a citizen inferior to a slave? Is an alien or one who owns some of his country's soil the best patriot? You have won by war most of your possessions, and hope to acquire the rest of the habitable globe. But now it is but a hazard whether you gain the rest by bravery or whether by your weakness and discords you are robbed of what you have by your foes. Wherefore, in prospect of such acquisitions, you should if need be spontaneously and of your own free will yield up these lands to those who will rear children for the service of the State. Do not sacrifice a great thing while striving for a small, especially as you are to receive no contemptible compensation for your expenditure on the land, in free ownership of 500 jugera secure for ever, and in case you have sons, of 250 more for each of them.

The striking point in the last extract is his remark about a 'small thing.' It is likely, enough that the losses of the proprietors as a body would not be overwhelming, and that the opposition was rendered furious almost as much by the principle of restitution, and interference with long-recognised ownership, as by the value of what they were called on to disgorge. Five hundred jugera of slave-tended pasture-land could not have been of very great importance to a rich Roman, who, however, might well have been alarmed by the warning of Gracchus with regard to the army, for in foreign service, and not in grazing or ploughing, the fine gentleman of the day found a royal road to wealth. [Grievances of the possessors.] On the other hand it is quite comprehensible both that the possessors imagined that they had a great grievance, and that they had some ground for their belief. A possessor, for instance, who had purchased from another in the full faith that his title would never be disturbed, had more right to be indignant than a proprietor of Indian stock would have, if in case of the bankruptcy of the Indian Government the British Government should refuse to refund his money. There must have been numbers of such cases with every possible complexity of title; and even if the class that would be actually affected was not large, it was powerful, and every landowner with a defective title would, however small his holding (provided it was over 30 jugera, the proposed allotment), take the alarm and help to swell the cry against the Tribune as a demagogue and a robber. This is what we can state about the agrarian law of Tiberius Gracchus. It remains to be told how it was carried.

[How the law was carried.] Gracchus had a colleague named Octavius, who is said to have been his personal friend. Octavius had land himself to lose if the law were carried, and he opposed it. Gracchus offered to pay him the value of the land out of his own purse; but Octavius was not to be so won over, and as Tribune interposed his veto to prevent the bill being read to the people that they might vote on it. Tiberius retorted by using his power to suspend public business and public payments. One day, when the people were going to vote, the other side seized the voting urns, and then Tiberius and the rest of the Tribunes agreed to take the opinion of the Senate. The result was that he came away more hopeless of success by constitutional means, and doubtless irritated by insult. He then proposed to Octavius that the people should vote whether he or Octavius should lose office—a weak proposal perhaps, but the proposal of an honest, generous man, whose aim was not self-aggrandisement but the public weal. Octavius naturally refused. Tiberius called together the thirty-five tribes, to vote whether or no Octavius should be deprived of his office. [Octavius deprived of the Tribunate.] The first tribe voted in the affirmative, and Gracchus implored Octavius even now to give way, but in vain. The next sixteen tribes recorded the same vote, and once more Gracchus interceded with his old friend. But he spoke to deaf ears. The voting went on, and when Octavius, on his Tribunate being taken from him, would not go away, Plutarch says that Tiberius ordered one of his freedmen to drag him from the Rostra. These acts of Tiberius Gracchus are commonly said to have been the beginning of revolution at Rome; and the guilt of it is accordingly laid at his door. And there can be no doubt that he was guilty in the sense that a man is guilty who introduces a light into some chamber filled with explosive vapour, which the stupidity or malice of others has suffered to accumulate. But, after all, too much is made of this violation of constitutional forms and the sanctity of the Tribunate. [Defence of the conduct of Gracchus.] The first were effete, and all regular means of renovating the Republic seemed to be closed to the despairing patriot, by stolid obstinacy sheltering itself under the garb of law and order. The second was no longer what it had been—the recognised refuge and defence of the poor. The rich, as Tiberius in effect argued, had found out how to use it also. If all men who set the example of forcible infringement of law are criminals, Gracchus was a criminal. But in the world's annals he sins in good company; and when men condemn him, they should condemn Washington also. Perhaps his failure has had most to do with his condemnation. Success justifies, failure condemns, most revolutions in most men's eyes. But if ever a revolution was excusable this was; for it was carried not by a small party for small aims, but by national acclamation, by the voices of Italians who flocked to Rome either to vote, or, if they had not votes themselves, to overawe those who had. How far Gracchus saw the inevitable effect of his acts is open to dispute. [Gracchus not a weak sentimentalist.] But probably he saw it as clearly as any man can see the future. Because he was generous and enthusiastic, it is assumed that he was sentimental and weak, and that his policy was guided by impulse rather than reason. There seems little to sustain such a judgment other than the desire of writers to emphasise a comparison between him and his brother. If his character had been what some say that it was, his speeches would hardly have been described by Cicero as acute and sensible, but not rhetorical enough. All his conduct was consistent. He strove hard and to the last to procure his end by peaceable means. Driven into a corner by the tactics of his opponents, he broke through the constitution, and once having done so, went the way on which his acts led him, without turning to the right hand or the left. There seems to be not a sign of his having drifted into revolution. Because a portrait is drawn in neutral tints, it does not follow that it is therefore faithful, and those writers who seem to think they must reconcile the fact of Tiberius having been so good a man with his having been, as they assert, so bad a citizen, have blurred the likeness in their anxiety about the chiaroscuro. No one would affirm that Tiberius committed no errors; but that he was a wise as well as a good man is far more in accordance with the facts than a more qualified verdict would be.

[Mean behaviour of the Senate.] The Senate showed its spite against the successful Tribune by petty annoyances, such as allowing him only about a shilling a day for his official expenditure, and, as rumour said, by the assassination of one of his friends. But, while men like P. Scipio Nasica busied themselves with such miserable tactics, Tiberius brought forward another great proposal supplementary to his agrarian law. [Proposal of Gracchus to distribute the legacy of Attalus.] Attalus, the last king of Pergamus, had just died and left his kingdom to Rome. Gracchus wished to divide his treasures among the new settlers, and expressed some other intention of transferring the settlement of the country from the Senate to the people. As to the second of these propositions it would be unsafe as well as unfair to Gracchus to pronounce judgment on it without a knowledge of its details. The first was both just and wise and necessary, for previous experience had shown that the first temptation of a pauper land-owner was to sell his land to the rich, and, as the law of Gracchus forbade this, he was bound to give the settler a fair start on his farm. [Retort of the Senate.] The Senate took fresh alarm, and it found vent again in characteristically mean devices. One senator said that a diadem and a purple robe had been brought to Gracchus from Pergamus. Another assailed him because men with torches escorted him home at night. Another twitted him with the deposition of Octavius. To this last attack, less contemptible than the others, he replied in a bold and able speech, which practically asserted that the spirit of the constitution was binding on a citizen, but that its letter under some circumstances was not.

[Other intended reforms of Gracchus.] He was also engaged in meditating other important reforms, all directed against the Senate's power. Plutarch says that they comprised abridgment of the soldier's term of service, an appeal to the people from the judices, and the equal partition between the Senate and equites of the privilege of serving as judices, which hitherto belonged only to the former. According to Velleius, Tiberius also promised the franchise to all Italians south of the Rubicon and the Macra, which, if true, is another proof of his far-seeing statesmanship. To carry out such extensive changes it was necessary to procure prolongation of office for himself, and he became a candidate for the next year's tribunate. [Gracchus stands again for the Tribunate. His motives.] To say that considerations of personal safety dictated his candidature is a very easy and specious insinuation, but is nothing more. It is indeed a good deal less, for it is utterly inconsistent with the other acts of an unselfish, dauntless career. At election-time the first two tribes voted for Tiberius. Then the aristocracy declared his candidature to be illegal because he could not hold office two years running. It may have been so, or the law may have been so violated as to be no more valid than the Licinian law, which, though never abrogated, had never much force. [Tactics of the Senate.] To fasten on some technical flaw in his procedure was precisely in keeping with the rest of the acts of the opposition. But those writers who accuse Tiberius of being guilty of another illegal act in standing fail to observe the force of the fact, that it was not till the first two tribes had voted that the aristocracy interfered. This shows that their objection was a last resort to an invalid statute, and a deed of which they were themselves ashamed. However, the president of the tribunes, Rubrius, hesitated to let the other tribes vote; and when Mummius, Octavius's substitute, asked Rubrius to yield to him the presidency, others objected that the post must be filled by lot, and so the election was adjourned till the next day.

It was clear enough to what end things were tending, and Tiberius, putting on mourning committed his young son to the protection of the people. It need hardly be said that the father's affection and the statesman's bitter dismay at finding the dearest object of his life about to be snatched from him by violence need not have been tinged with one particle of personal fear. A man of tried bravery like Gracchus might guard his own life indeed, but only as be regarded it as indispensable to a great cause. That evening he told his partisans he would give them a sign next day if he should think it necessary to use force at his election. It has been assumed that this proves he was meditating treason. But it proves no more than that he meant to repel force

forcibly if, as was only too certain, force should be used, and this is not treason. No other course was open to him. The one weak spot in his policy was that he had no material strength at his back. Even Sulla would have been a lost man at a later time, if he had not had an army at hand to which he could flee for refuge, just as without the army Cromwell would have been powerless. But it was harvest-time now, and the rural allies of Gracchus were away from home in the fields. [Murder of Gracchus.] The next day dawned, and with it occurred omens full of meaning to the superstitious Romans. The sacred fowls would not feed. Tiberius stumbled at the doorway of his house and broke the nail of his great toe. Some crows fought on the roof of a house on the left hand, and one dislodged a tile, which fell at his feet. But Blossius was at his side encouraging him, and Gracchus went on to the Capitol and was greeted with a great cheer by his partisans. [Different accounts given by Appian and Plutarch.] Appian says that when the rich would not allow the election to proceed, Tiberius gave the signal. Plutarch tells us that Fulvius Flaccus came and told him that his foes had resolved to slay him, and, having failed to induce the consul Scaevola to act, were arming their friends and slaves, and that Gracchus gave the signal then. As Appian agrees with Plutarch in his account of Nasica's conduct in the Senate, the last is the more probable version of what occurred. Nasica called on Scaevola to put down the tyrant. Scaevola replied that he would not be the first to use force. Then Nasica, calling on the senators to follow him, mounted the Capitol to a position above that of Gracchus. Arming themselves with clubs and legs of benches, his followers charged down and dispersed the crowd. Gracchus stumbled over some prostrate bodies, and was slain either by a blow from P. Satyreius, a fellow-tribune, or from L. Rufus, for both claimed the distinction. So died a genuine patriot and martyr; and so foul a murder fitly heralded the long years of bloodshed and violence which were in store for the country which he died to save.
* * * * *

CHAPTER III.CAIUS GRACCHUS.

Over three hundred of the people were killed and thrown into the Tiber, and the aristocracy followed up their triumph as harshly as they dared. They banished some, and slew others of the tribune's partisans. Plutarch says that they fastened up one in a chest with vipers. When Blossius was brought before his judges he avowed that he would have burned the Capitol if Gracchus had told him to do it, so confident was he in his leader's patriotism—an answer testifying not only to the nobleness of the two friends, but to the strong character of one of them. Philosophers are not so impressed by weak, impulsive men. Blossius was spared, probably because he had connexions with some of the nobles rather than because his reply inspired respect. But while the aristocracy was making war on individuals, the work of the dead man went on, as if even from the grave he was destined to bring into sharper relief the pettiness of their projects by the grandeur of his own. [The law of Gracchus remains in force.] The allotment of land was vigorously carried out; and when Appius Claudius and Mucianus died, the commissioners were partisans of Tiberius—his brother Caius, M. Fulvius Flaccus, and C. Papirius Carbo. [Its beneficial effects.] In the year 125, instead of another decrease in the able-bodied population, we find an increase of nearly 80,000. It seems probable that this increase was solely in consequence of what the allotment commissioners did for the Roman burgesses. Nor, if the Proletarii and Capite Censi were not included in the register of those classed for military service, is the increase remarkable, for it would be to members of those classes that the allotments would be chiefly assigned. Moreover, the poor whom the rich expelled from their lands did not give in their names to the censors, and did not attend to the education of their children. These men would, on receiving allotments, enrol themselves. The consul of the year 132 inscribed on a public monument that he was the first who had turned the shepherds out of the domains, and installed farmers in their stead; and these farmers became, as Gracchus intended, a strong reinforcement to the Roman soldier-class, as well as a check to slave labour. What was done at Rome was done also, it is said, throughout Italy, and if on the same scale, it must have been a really enormous measure of relief to the poor, and a vast stride towards a return to a healthier tenure of the land. [Difficulties and hardships in enforcing it.] But it is not hard to imagine what heart-burnings the commissioners must have aroused. Some men were thrust out of tilled land on to waste land. Some who thought that their property was private property found to their cost that it was the State's. Some had encroached, and their encroachments were now exposed. Some of the Socii had bought parcels of the land, and found out now that they had no title. Lastly, some land had been by special decrees assigned to individual states, and the commissioners at length proceeded to stretch out their hands towards it.

Historians, while recording such things, have failed to explain why the chief opposition to the commissioners arose from the country which had furnished the chief supporters of Tiberius, and what was the exact attitude assumed by Scipio Aemilianus. It is lost sight of that as at Rome there were two classes, so there were two classes in Italy. It is absurd constantly to put prominently forward the sharp division of interests in the capital, and then speak of the country classes as if they were all one body, and their interests the same. [Divisions in Italy similar to those in Rome.] The natural and apparently the only way of explaining what at first sight seems the inconsistency of the country class is to conclude, that the men who supported Tiberius were the poor of the Italian towns and the small farmers of the country, while the men who called on Scipio to save them from the commissioners were the capitalists of the towns and the richer farmers—some of them voters, some of them non-voters—with their forces swollen, it may be, by not a few who, having clamoured for more land, found now that the title to what they already had was called in question. Though this cannot be stated as a certainty, it at least accounts for what historians, after many pages on the subject, have left absolutely unexplained, and it presents the conduct of Scipio Aemilianus in quite a different light from the one in which it has commonly been regarded. He is usually extolled as a patriot who would not stir to humour a Roman rabble, but who, when downtrodden honest farmers, his comrades in the wars, appealed to him, at once stepped into the arena as their champion. [Attitude of Scipio Aemilianus.] In reality he was a reactionist who, when the inevitable results of those liberal ideas which had been broached in his own circle stared him in the face, seized the first available means of stifling them. The world had moved too fast for him. As censor, instead of beseeching the gods to increase the glory of the State, he begged them to preserve it. And no doubt he would have greatly preferred that the gods should act without his intervention. Brave as a man, he was a pusillanimous statesman; and when confronted by the revolutionary spirit which he and his friends had helped to evoke, he determined at all costs to prop up the senatorial power. [His unpopularity with the Senate.] But the Senate hated him, partly as a trimmer, and partly because by his personal character he rebuked their baseness. He had just impeached Aurelius Cotta, a senator, and the judices, from spite against him, had refused to convict. So he turned to the Italian land-owners, and became the mouthpiece of their selfishness, for a selfish or at best a narrow-minded end. The nobles must have, at heart, disliked his allies; but they cheered him in the Senate, and he succeeded in practically strangling the commission by procuring the transfer of its jurisdiction to the consuls. The consul for the time being immediately found a pretext for leaving Rome, and a short time afterwards Scipio was found one morning dead in his bed. [His death.] He had gone to his chamber the night before to think over what he should say next day to the people about the position of the country class, and, if he was murdered, it is almost as probable that he was murdered by some rancorous foe in the Senate as by Carbo or any other Gracchan. It was well for his reputation that he died just then. Without Sulla's personal vices he might have played Sulla's part as a politician, and his atrocities in Spain as well as his remark on the death of Tiberius Gracchus—words breathing the very essence of a narrow swordsman's nature—showed that from bloodshed at all events he would not have shrunk. It is hard to respect such a man in spite of all his good qualities. Fortune gave him the opportunity of playing a great part, and he shrank from it. When the crop sprang up which he had himself helped to sow, he blighted it. But because he was personally respectable, and because he held a middle course between contemporary parties, he has found favour with historians, who are too apt to forget that there is in politics, as in other things, a right course and a wrong, and that to attempt to walk along both at once proves a man to be a weak statesman, and does not prove him to be a great or good man.

[The early career of Caius Gracchus.] In B.C. 126 Caius Gracchus, seven years after he had been made one of the commissioners for the allotment of public land, was elected quaestor. Sardinia was at that time in rebellion, and it fell by lot to Caius to go there as quaestor to the consul Orestes. It is said that he kept quiet when Tiberius was killed, and intended to steer clear of politics. But one of those splendid bursts of oratory, with which he had already electrified the people, remains to show over what he was for ever brooding. 'They slew him,' he cried, 'these scoundrels slew Tiberius, my noble brother! Ah, they are all of one pattern.' He said this in advocating the Lex Papiria, which proposed to make the re-election of a tribune legal. But Scipio opposed the law, and it was defeated then, to be carried, however, a few years later. Again, in the year of his quaestorship, he spoke against the law of M. Junius Pennus, which aimed at expelling all Peregrini from Rome. They were the very men by whose help Tiberius had carried his agrarian law, and when Caius spoke for them he was clearly treading in his brother's steps. At a later time he declared that he dreamt Tiberius came to him and said, 'Why do you hesitate? You cannot escape your doom and mine—to live for the people and die for them.' Such a story would be effective in a speech, and particularly effective when told to a superstitious audience; but his day-dreams we may be sure were the cause and not the consequence of his visions of the night. For there can be no doubt that the younger brother had already one purpose and one only—to avenge the death of Tiberius and carry out his designs.

Such omens as Roman credulity fastened on when the political air was heavy with coming storm abounded now. With grave irony the historian records: 'Besides showers of oil and milk in the neighbourhood of Veii, a fact of which some people may doubt, an owl, it is said, was seen on the Capitol, which may have been true.' Fulvius Flaccus, the friend of Gracchus, made the first move. [Proposition of Fulvius Flaccus. Its significance.] In order to buy off the opposition of the Socii to the agrarian law, he proposed to give them the franchise, just as Licinius, when he had offered the poor plebeians a material boon, offered the rich ones a political one, so as to secure the united support of the whole body. The proposal was significant, and it was made at a critical time. The poor Italians were chafing, no doubt, at the suspension of the agrarian law. The rich were indignant at the carrying of the law of Pennus. Other and deeper causes of irritation have been mentioned above. In the year of the proposal of Flaccus, and very likely in consequence of its rejection, Fregellae—a Latin colony—revolted. [Revolt and punishment of Fregellae.] The revolt was punished with the ferocity of panic. The town was destroyed; a Roman colony, Fabrateria, was planted near its site; and for the moment Italian discontent was awed into sullen silence. No wonder the Senate was panic-stricken. Here was a real omen, not conjured up by superstition, that one of those towns, which through Rome's darkest fortunes in the second Punic War had remained faithful to her, should single-handed and in time of peace raise the standard of rebellion. Was Fregellae indeed single-handed? The Senate suspected not, and turned furiously on the Gracchan party, and, it is alleged, accused Caius of complicity with the revolt. [Caius Gracchus accused of treason. He stands for the tribunate.] It was rash provocation to give to such a man at such a time. If he was accused, he was acquitted, and he at once stood for the tribunate. Thus the party which had slain his brother found itself again at death-grips with an even abler and more implacable foe.

[Prominence of Gracchus at home and abroad.] There is no doubt that for some time past Caius Gracchus, young as he was, and having as yet filled none of the regular high offices, had had the first place in all men's thoughts. His first speech had been received by the people with wild delight. He was already the greatest orator in Rome. His importance is shown by the Senate's actually prolonging the consul's command, in order to keep his quaestor longer abroad. But his friends were consoled for his absence by the stories they heard of the respect shown to him by foreign nations. The Sardinians would not grant supplies to Orestes, and the Senate approved their refusal. But Gracchus interposed, and they voluntarily gave what they had before appealed against. Micipsa, son of Masinissa, also sent corn to Orestes, but averred that it was out of respect to Gracchus. The Senate's fears and the esteem of foreigners were equally just. What the life of Gracchus was in Sardinia he has himself told us; and from the implied contrast we may judge what was the life of the nobles of the time. [His description of the life of a noble.] 'My life,' he said to the people, 'in the province was not planned to suit my ambition, but your interests. There was no gormandising with me, no handsome slaves in waiting, and at my table your sons saw more seemliness than at head-quarters. No man can say without lying that I ever took a farthing as a present or put anyone to expense. I was there two years; and if a single courtesan ever crossed my doors, or if proposals from me were ever made to anyone's slave-pet, set me down for the vilest and most infamous of men. And if I was so scrupulous towards slaves, you may judge what my life must have been with your sons. And, citizens, here is the fruit of such a life. I left Rome with a full purse and have brought it back empty. Others took out their wine jars full of wine, and brought them back full of money.'

Such was the man who now came back to Rome to demand from the aristocracy a reckoning for which he had been yearning with undying passion for nearly ten years. An exaggerated contrast between him and Tiberius at the expense of the latter has been previously condemned. The man who originates is always so far greater than the man who imitates, and Caius only followed where his brother led. He was not greater than but only like his brother in his bravery, in his culture, in the faculty of inspiring in his friends strong enthusiasm and devotion, in his unswerving pursuit of a definite object, and, as his sending the son of Fulvius Flaccus to the Senate just before his death proves in the teeth of all assertions to the contrary, in his willingness to use his personal influence in order to avoid civil bloodshed. [Caius compared with Tiberius.] The very dream which Caius told to the people shows that his brother's spell was still on him, and his telling it, together with his impetuous oratory and his avowed fatalism, militates against the theory that Tiberius was swayed by impulse and sentiment, and he by calculation and reason. But no doubt he profited by experience of the past. He had learned how to bide his time, and to think generosity wasted on the murderous crew whom he had sworn to punish. Pure in life, perfectly prepared for a death to which he considered himself foredoomed, glowing with one fervent passion, he took up his brother's cause with a double portion of his brother's spirit, because he had thought more before action, because he had greater natural eloquence, and because being forewarned he was forearmed.

In spite of the labours of recent historians, the legislation of Caius Gracchus is still hard to understand. Where the original authorities contradict each other, as they often do, probable conjecture is the most which can be attained, and no attempt will be made here to specify what were the measures of the first tribunate of Caius and what of the second. [The general purpose of the legislation of Caius.] The general scope and tendency of his legislation is clear enough. It was to overthrow the senatorial government, and in the new government to give the chief share of the executive power to the mercantile class, and the chief share of the legislative power to the country class. These were his immediate aims. Probably he meant to keep all the strings he thus set in motion in his own hands, so as to be practically monarch of Rome. But whether he definitely conceived the idea of monarchy, and, looking beyond his own requirements, pictured to himself a successor at some future time inheriting the authority which he had established, no one can say. In such vast schemes there must have been much that was merely tentative. But had he lived and retained his influence we may be sure that the Empire would have been established a century earlier than it was.

[Date of the tribunate of Caius, December 10, B.C. 124.] Rome was thronged to overflowing by the country class, and the nobles strained every nerve in opposition when Caius was elected tribune. He was only fourth on the list out of ten, and entered on his office on December 10, B.C. 124. With a fixed presentiment of his own fate, he felt that, even if he wished to remain passive, the people would not permit him to be so. He might, he said, have pleaded that he and his young child were the last representatives of a noble line—of P. Africanus and Tiberius Gracchus—and that he had lost a brother in the people's cause; but the people would not have listened to the plea. It has been said that his mother dissuaded him from his intentions. But the fragments on which the statement is based are as likely as not spurious; and Cornelia's fortitude after she had lost both her sons would hardly have been shown by one capable of subordinating public to private interests.

[Story of his mother's sentiments.] It is far more likely that when in his stirring speeches he spoke of his home as no place for him to visit, while his mother was weeping and in despair, he was influenced by her adjurations to avenge his brother, and not by any craven warnings against sharing his fate. However this may have been, no timid influences could be traced in the fiery passion of his first speeches. [Story of the means by which he modulated his voice when speaking.] He was, in fact, so carried away by his feelings that he had to resort to a curious device in order to keep his voice under control. A man with a musical instrument used, it is said, to stand near him, and warn him by a note at times if he was pitching his voice too high or too low. It was now that he told his stories of the flogging of the magistrate of Teanum and the murder of the Venusian herdsman, and we can imagine how they would incense his hearers against the nobles. Against one of them, Octavius, he specially directed a law, making it illegal for any magistrate previously deposed by the people to be elected to office; but this, at Cornelia's suggestion it is said, he withdrew. Another law also had special reference to the fate of Tiberius. It made illegal the trial of any citizen for an offence which involved the loss of his civic rights without the consent of the people. [Caius procures the banishment of Popillius Laenas.] This law, if in force, would have prevented the ferocity with which Popillius Laenas hunted down the partisans of Tiberius; and Caius followed it up according to the oration De Domo, by procuring against Popillius a sentence of outlawry. One of the fragments from his speeches was probably spoken at this time. In it he told the people that they now had the chance they had so long and so passionately desired; and that, if they did not avail themselves of it, they would lay themselves open to the charge of caprice or of ungoverned temper. Popillius anticipated the sentence by voluntary retirement from Rome.

[His Lex Frumentaria.] Having satisfied his conscience by the performance of what no doubt seemed to him sacred duties, Caius at once set to work to build up his new constitution. It is commonly represented that in order to gain over the people to his side he cynically bribed them by his Lex Frumentaria. Now if this were true, and Caius were as clear-sighted as the same writers who insist on the badness of the law describe him to have been, it is hard to see how they can in the same breath eulogise his goodness and nobleness. To gain his ends he would have been using vile means, and would have been a vile man. [The common criticism on it unjust.] Looking, however, more closely into the law, we are led to doubt whether it was bad, or, at all events, even granting that eventually it led to evil, whether it would have appeared likely to do so to Caius. The public land, it must be remembered, was liable to an impost called vectigal. This vectigal went into the Aerarium, which the nobles had at their disposal. Now the law of Caius appears to have fixed a nominal price for corn to all Roman citizens, and if the market price was above this price the difference would have to be made good from the Aerarium. We at once see the object of Caius, and how the justice of it might have blinded him to the demoralising effects of his measure. 'The public land,' he said in effect, 'belongs to all Romans and so does the vectigal. If you take that to which you have no right, you shall give it back again in cheap corn.' In short, it was a clever device for partially neutralising the long misappropriation of the State's property by the nobles, and for giving to the people what belonged to the people—to each man, as it were, so many ears of corn from whatever fraction would be his own share of the land. [Contrast between the just proposal of Caius and the demagogy of Drusus.] When Drusus was afterwards set up to outbid Caius, he proposed that the vectigal should be remitted, and that the land that had been assigned might be sold by the occupier. How this would catch the farmer's fancy is as obvious as is its odious dishonesty. It was dishonest to the State because it was only fair that each occupier should contribute to its funds, and because it did away with the hope of filling Italy with free husbandmen. It was dishonest to the occupier himself, because it put in his way the worst temptation to unthriftiness. When Caius renewed his brother's laws he purposely charged the land distributed to the poor with a yearly vectigal. How different was this from the mere demagogic trick of Drusus! It appears, then, that the Lex Frumentaria of Caius is not the indefensible measure which modern writers, filled with modern notions, have called it. It has, moreover, been well said that it was a kind of poor-law; and, even if bad in itself, may have been the least bad remedy for the pauperism which not Caius, but senatorial misgovernment had brought about. No doubt it conferred popularity on Caius, and no doubt his popularity was acceptable to him; but there is no ground for believing that his noble nature deliberately stooped to demoralise the mob for selfish motives.

[His Lex Judiciaria.] One great party, however, he had thus won over to his side. The Lex Judiciaria gained over the equites also. It has been before explained that the equites at this time were non-senatorial rich men. Senators were forbidden by law to mix in commerce, though no doubt they evaded the law. Between the senatorial and moneyed class there was a natural ill-will, which Caius proceeded to use and increase. His exact procedure we do not know for certain. According to some authorities he made the judices eligible from the equites only, instead of from the Senate. In the epitome of Livy it is stated that 600 of the equites were to be added to the number of the senators, so that the equites should have twice as much power as the Senate itself.

This at first sight seems nonsense. But Caius may have proposed that for judicial purposes 600 equites should form, as it were, a second chamber, which, being twice as numerous, would permit two judices for every senatorial judex. In form he may have devised that 'counter-senate,' which, as it has been shown, he in fact created. [The effects of it. The Senate abased, the equites exalted.] But whether Caius provided that all the judices or only two-thirds of them should be chosen from the equites, and in whatever way he did so, he did succeed in exalting the moneyed class and abasing the Senate. In civil processes, and in the permanent and temporary commissions for the administration of justice, the equites were henceforth supreme. Even the senators themselves depended on their verdict for acquittal or condemnation, and the chief power in the State had changed hands. Of course the change would not be felt at once to the full; but this was the most trenchant stroke which Gracchus aimed at the Senate's power. Here, again, it is customary to write of his actions as if they were governed solely by feeling, quite apart from all considerations of right and wrong. But Cicero declares that for nearly fifty years, while the equites discharged this office, there was not even the slightest suspicion of a single eques being bribed in his capacity as judex; and after every allowance has been made for Ciceronian exaggeration, the statement may at least warrant us in believing that Gracchus had some reason for hoping that his change would be a change for the better, even if, as Appian declares, it turned out in the end just the opposite. Indeed, it is beyond question that, as the provinces were governed by the senatorial class, judices who had to decide cases like those of Cotta would be more fairly chosen from the equites than from the class to which Cotta belonged.

[The taxation of Asia.] We know little of the arrangements for the taxation of Asia made by Gracchus. He provided that the taxes should be let by auction at Rome, which would undoubtedly be a boon to the Roman capitalists and a check to provincial competition. He is said also to have substituted the whole system of direct and indirect taxes for the previously existing system of fixed payments by the various states. There was a certain narrowness about the conceptions of both the Gracchi with regard to the transmarine world, which was common to all Romans; to which, for instance, Tiberius gave expression when he spoke of the conquest of the whole world as a thing which his audience had a right to expect; and this sentiment may have in this instance influenced Caius to use harshness. [The common criticism on the measure of Caius unjust.] But even here to condemn without more knowledge of his measures would be unjust. Fixed payments it must be remembered were not always preferable to tithes of the produce. In a sterile year the payers of vectigalia would be best off. Again, if a rich province like Asia did not pay tribute in proportion to other provinces, a re-adjustment of its taxes would not seem to the Romans unfair; and perhaps auction at Rome would after all be less mischievous than a hole-and-corner arrangement in the provinces. If the sheep were to be fleeced, they would not be shorn closest in the capital. [Measure for the relief of publicani.] To another of his provisions at all events no one could object—the one which gave relief to such publicani as had suffered loss in collecting the revenue.

[Alleged privileges conferred on the equites.] Gracchus had thus raised the equites above the Senate at Rome in the courts of justice, and opened a golden harvest to them in the provinces. It is conjectured that he also gave them the distinction of a golden finger-ring and reserved seats at the public spectacles. Two classes were thus gratified, the city poor and the city rich. [Caius attempts to conciliate the farmer class and the Italians.] But Gracchus had to deal also with those of the country class in whose favour his brother's agrarian law had been passed, and with those who had resented the law. To provide for the former he renewed the operation of his brother's law, which had been suspended by Scipio's intervention, and probably took away its administrations from the consuls and restored it to triumvirs; and as that might be insufficient, he began the establishment of many colonies in various parts of the peninsula; and even beyond it at Carthage, to which he invited colonists from all parts of Italy. To compensate and benefit the latter he proposed to give them the franchise, so as to secure them from such outrages as that of Teanum. For though such of them as belonged to Roman colonies or municipia possessed the franchise already, the mass of the Latins and Italians did not possess it. There are different accounts of this measure; but Appian says that he wished to give the Latini the Jus Suffragii and Jus Honorum, and to the rest of the Italians the Jus Suffragii only. But here he reckoned without his host. [Feeling at Rome.] The boons of colonies and cheap bread, and the prospect of a slice out of the public land occupied by Italians, were all not strong enough to overcome the deep, ingrained prejudice against extending the franchise. Rich and poor Romans met here on the common ground of narrow pride, and the offence caused by this wise project probably paved the way for the tribune's fall.

In speaking of the motives which induced Tiberius to seek the tribunate a second time (p. 33) it has been said that he was not influenced by personal considerations, but wanted time to carry out his measures. This view is confirmed by what Appian says about Caius, namely, that he was elected a second time; for already a law had been enacted to this effect, that if a tribune could not find time for executing in his tribunate what he had promised, the people might give the office to him again in preference to anyone else. This has been pronounced to be a blunder on Appian's part, but without adequate reason. It was in fact the natural and inevitable law which Caius would insist on first, and he would plead for it precisely on the grounds which Appian states. It is also clear that such a law once passed made virtual monarchy at Rome possible. [Other measures of Caius.] In fact the other measures of Caius were both worthy of a great and wise monarch, and might with good reason be thought to be designed to lead to monarchy. [Roads. Granaries. Soldiers' uniform. Age for service.] He constructed magnificent roads—along which, it would be whispered, his voters might come more easily to Rome. He built public granaries. He gave the soldiers clothing at the cost of the State. He made seventeen the minimum age for service in the army. He himself superintended the plantation of his own colonies. Everywhere he made his finger felt; but whether this was of set purpose or only from his constitutional energy it is hard to decide. His chief object, however, was to overthrow the Senate; and we have not yet exhausted the list of his assaults upon it. [Change in nomination to provinces.] Hitherto it had been the custom for the Senate to name the consular provinces for the next year after the election of the consuls, which meant that if a favourite was consul a rich province was given to him, and if not, a poor one. Caius enacted that the consular provinces should be named before the election of the consuls. By way, perhaps, of softening this restriction he took away from the tribunes their veto on the naming of the consular provinces. [Alleged change in the order of voting.] He is further supposed, though on slender evidence, to have changed the order of voting in the Comitia Centuriata. Formerly the first class voted first. Now the order of voting first was to be settled by lot, and so the influence of the rich would be diminished.

[General criticism of his schemes.] Such, in outline, was the grand scheme of Caius Gracchus. If he was less single-minded in his aims than his brother, he could hardly help being so; and, having to reconcile so many conflicting interests, he may have swerved from what would have been his own ideal. But that his main purpose was to break down a rotten system, and establish a sound one on its ruins, and that no petty motive of expediency guided him, but only the one principle, 'salus populi suprema lex,' is incontrovertible. When we think of him so eloquent, resolute, and energetic, conceiving such great projects and executing them in person, making the regeneration of his country his lodestar in spite of his ever-present belief that he would, in the end, fall by the same fate as his brother, we think of him as one of the noblest figures in history—a purer and less selfish Julius Caesar.

[Machinations of the nobles.] As the petty acts of the nobles had brought out into relief the large policy of Tiberius, so it was now. They resorted to even lower tricks than accusations of tyranny, and found in the fatuity or dishonesty of Drusus a tool even more effective than Nasica's brutality. The plantation of a colony at Carthage was looked at askance by many Romans. It was the first colony planted out of Italy, and the superstitious were filled with forebodings which the Senate eagerly exaggerated. Such colonies had repeatedly out-grown and overtopped the parent state. The ground had been solemnly cursed, and the restoration of the town forbidden. When the first standard was set up by the colonists a blast of wind, it is said, blew it down, and scattered the flesh of the victims; and wolves had torn up the stakes that marked out the site. Such malicious stories met with readier credence, because, if it is true that Caius had called for colonists from all Italy, and Junonia was to be a Roman colony, he was evading the decree of the people against extending the franchise; and he was thus admitting to it, by a side-wind, those to whom it had just in the harshest manner been refused. For, when the vote had been taken, every man not having a vote had been expelled from the city, and forbidden to come within five miles of it till the voting was over. Caius had come to live in the Forum instead of on the Palatine when he returned to Rome, among his friends as he thought; and still even in little matters he stood forward as the champion of the poor against the rich. There was going to be a show of gladiators in the Forum, and the magistrates had enclosed the arena with benches, which they meant to hire out. Caius asked them to remove the benches, and, on their refusal, went the night before the show and took them all away. Anyone who has witnessed modern athletic sports, and observed how a crowd will hem in the competitors so that only a few spectators can see, although an equally good view can be obtained by a great number if the ring is enlarged, will perceive Caius's object, and be slow to admit that he spoiled the show. But though such acts pleased the people, all of them had not forgiven him the proposition about the franchise; and his popularity was on the wane. [Drusus outbids Caius.] The Senate had suborned one of his colleagues, M. Livius Drusus, to outbid him. Either Drusus thought he was guiding the Senate into a larger policy when he was himself merely the Senate's puppet, and this his son's career makes probable, or he was cynically dishonest and unscrupulous.

Caius had meditated, it may be, many colonies, but, according to Plutarch, had at this time only actually settled two. Drusus proposed to plant twelve, each of 3,000 citizens. Caius had superintended the settlement himself, and employed his friends. With virtuous self-denial Drusus washed his hands of all such patronage. Caius had imposed a yearly tax on those to whom he gave land; Drusus proposed to remit it. Caius had wished to give the Latins the franchise; Drusus replied by a comparatively ridiculous favour, which, however, might appeal more directly to the lower class of Latins. No Latin, he said, should be liable to be flogged even when serving in the army. Drusus could afford to be liberal. His colonies were sham colonies. His remission of the vectigal was a thin-coated poison. His promise to the Latins was at best a cheap one, and was not carried out. But none the less his treachery or imbecility served its purpose, and the greedier and baser of the partisans of Gracchus began to look coldly on their leader. [Caius rejected for the tribunate.] It is stated, indeed, that on his standing for the tribunate a third time he was rejected by fraud, his colleagues having made a false return of the names of the candidates. In any case he was not elected, and one of the consuls for the year 121 was L. Opimius, his mortal foe.

The end was drawing near. Sadly Caius must have recognised that his presentiments would soon be fulfilled, and that he must share his brother's fate. [Preparations for civil strife.] His foes proposed to repeal the law for the settlement of Junonia, and, according to Plutarch, others of his laws also. Warned by the past, his friends armed. Men came disguised as reapers to defend him. It is likely enough that they were really reapers, who would remember why Tiberius lost his life, and that their support would have saved him. Fulvius was addressing the people about the law when Caius, attended by some of his partisans, came to the Capitol. He did not join the meeting, but began walking up and down under a colonnade to wait its issue. Here a man named Antyllus, who was sacrificing, probably in behalf of Opimius the consul, either insulted the Gracchans and was stabbed by them, or caught hold of Caius's hand, or by some other familiarity or importunity provoked some hasty word or gesture from him, upon which he was stabbed by a servant. As soon as the deed was done the people ran away, and Caius hastened to the assembly to explain the affair. But it began to rain heavily; and for this, and because of the murder, the assembly was adjourned. Caius and Fulvius went home; but that night the people thronged the Forum, expecting that some violence would be done at daybreak. Opimius was not slow to seize the opportunity. He convoked the Senate, and occupied the temple of Castor and Pollux with armed men. The body of Antyllus was placed on a bier, and with loud lamentations borne along the Forum; and as it passed by the senators came out and hypocritically expressed their anger at the deed. Then, going indoors, they authorised the consul, by the usual formula, to resort to arms. He summoned the senators and equites to arm, and each eques was to bring two armed slaves. The equites owed much to Gracchus, but they basely deserted him now. Fulvius, on his side, armed and prepared for a struggle. All the night the friends of Caius guarded his door, watching and sleeping by turns. [Fighting in Rome.] The house of Fulvius was also surrounded by men, who drank and bragged of what they would do on the morrow, and Fulvius is said to have set them the example. At daybreak he and his men, to whom he distributed the arms which he had when consul taken from the Gauls, rushed shouting up to the Aventine and seized it. Caius said good-bye to his wife and little child, and followed, in his toga, and unarmed. He knew he was going to his death, but

  For his country felt alone,
  And prized her blood beyond his own.

One effort he made to avert the struggle. He induced Fulvius to send his young son to the Senate to ask for terms. The messenger returned with the Senate's reply that they must lay down their arms, and the two leaders must come and answer for their acts. Caius was ready to go. But Fulvius was too deeply committed, and sent his son back again, upon which Opimius seized him, and at once marched to the Aventine. There was a fight, in which Fulvius was beaten, and with another son fled and hid himself in a bath or workshop. His pursuers threatened to burn all that quarter if he was not given up; so the man who had admitted him told another man to betray him, and father and son were slain.

[Murder of Caius.] Meanwhile Caius, who had neither armed nor fought, was about to kill himself in the temple of Diana, when his two friends implored him to try and save himself for happier times. Then it is said he invoked a curse on the people for their ingratitude, and fled across the Tiber. He was nearly overtaken; but his two staunch friends, Pomponius and Laetorius, gave their lives for their leader—Pomponius at the Porta Trigemina below the Aventine, Laetorius in guarding the bridge which was the scene of the feat of Horatius Cocles. As Caius passed people cheered him on, as if it was a race in the games. He called for help, but no one helped him—for a horse, but there was none at hand. One slave still kept up with him, named Philocrates or Euporus. Hard pressed by their pursuers the two entered the grove of

Furina, and there the slave first slew Caius and then himself. A wretch named Septimuleius cut off the head of Gracchus; for a proclamation had been made that whosoever brought the heads of the two leaders should receive their weight in gold. Septimuleius, it is said, took out the brains and filled the cavity with lead; but if he cheated Opimius, Opimius in his turn cheated those who brought the head of Fulvius, for as they were of the lower class he would pay them nothing. The story may be false; but Opimius was subsequently convicted of selling his country's interests to Jugurtha for money, so that with equal likelihood it may be true. In the fight and afterwards he put to death 3,000 men, many of whom were innocent, but whom he would not allow to speak in their defence. The houses of Caius and Fulvius were sacked, and the property of the slain was confiscated. Then the city was purified, and the ferocious knave Opimius raised a temple to Concord, on which one night was found written 'The work of Discord makes the temple of Concord.' That year there was a famous vintage, and nearly two centuries afterwards there was some wine which had been made at the time that Caius Gracchus died. The wine, says the elder Pliny, tasted like and had the consistency of bitterish honey. But the memory of the great tribune has lasted longer than the wine, and will be honoured for ever by all those who revere patriotism and admire genius. He for whom at the last extremity friend and slave give their lives does not fall ingloriously. Even for a life so noble such deaths are a sufficient crown.

[The mother of the Gracchi.] The child of Caius did not long survive him. The son of Tiberius died while a boy. Only Cornelia, the worthy mother of the heroic brothers, remained. She could (according to the purport of Plutarch's pathetic narrative) speak of them without a sigh or tear; and those who concluded from this that her mind was clouded by age or misfortune, were too dull themselves to comprehend how a noble nature and noble training can support sorrow, for though fate may often frustrate virtue, yet 'to bear is to conquer our fate.'

[Position of the nobles after the murder. Lex Maria.] The nobles no doubt thought that, having got rid of Gracchus, they had renewed their own lease of power. But they had only placed themselves at the mercy of meaner men. The murderous scenes just related happened in 121 B.C., and in 119 we read of a Lex Maria, the first law, that is to say, promulgated by the destined scourge of the Roman aristocracy. Every Roman could vote, and voted by ballot, and was eligible to every office. The first law of Marius was to protect voters from the solicitations of candidates for office. It is significant that the nobles opposed it, though in the end it was carried. Stealthy intrigue was now their safest weapon, but their power was tottering to its fall. Too jealous of each other to submit to the supremacy of one, it only remained for them to be overthrown by some leader of the popular party, and the Republic was no more. Yet, as if smitten by judicial blindness, they proceeded to hasten on their own ruin by reactionary provocations to their opponents. [Gracchan laws remain in force.] They dared not interfere with the corn law of Caius, for now that every man had a vote, which he could give by ballot, they were dependent on the suffrages of the mob. Neither dared they till seventeen years later make an attempt to interfere with the selection of the judices from the equestrian order, and even then the attempt failed. The scheme of taxation in the province of Asia was also left untouched. But what they dared to do they did. They prosecuted the adherents of Gracchus. They recalled Popillius from exile. When Opimius was arraigned for 'perduellio,' or misuse of his official power to compass the death of a citizen, they procured his acquittal. But when Carbo was accused of the same crime, they remembered that he had been a partisan of Tiberius, though since a renegade, and would not help him. So while Opimius got off, the champion of Opimius was driven to commit suicide—a fitting close to a contemptible career.

[Reactionary legislation.] But they soon assailed measures as well as men. The Lex Baebia appears to have secured those who had actually established themselves at Carthage in their allotments; but the Senate annulled the colonies which Caius had planned in Italy, and, with one exception, Neptunia, broke up those already settled. [The agrarian law annulled.] Then by three successive enactments it got rid of the agrarian law, and plunged Italy again into the decline from which by the help of that law she was emerging. 1. The occupiers were allowed again to sell their land. Tiberius had expressly forbidden this, and now the rich at once began to buy out the small owners, whom they often evicted by means more or less foul. 2. A tribune named Borius, or Thorius, prohibited any further distribution of land, thus knocking on the head the permanent commission. These two laws were tantamount to handing over to the rich in the city and the country the greater part of the public land, giving them a legal title to it instead of the possession on sufferance with which the Gracchi had interfered. The mouths of the farmers were stopped by the pernicious but tempting permission to sell their land. The people were cajoled by the vectigalia, which Drusus had abolished, being reimposed, and the proceeds divided among them. 3. Encouraged by the general acquiescence in these insidious aggressions they induced a tribune, whose name is conjectured to have been C. Baebius, to do away with the vectigalia altogether. [Lex Thoria.] The date of this law, usually called the Thorian law, was 111 B.C. The real Thorian law was probably carried in 118 B.C. Between these dates the rich would have been getting back the land from the poor occupiers, and so, when the Senate abolished the vectigalia, it was really pocketing them, and once for all and by a legal form turning the public into private land. This law, which is here called the Baebian law, Cicero ascribes to Spurius Thorius, who, he says, freed the land from the vectigal. But as Appian says that Spurius Borius imposed the vectigal, it is assumed that Cicero confused names, that the Spurius Borius of Appian was Spurius Thorius, and that the tribune whom Cicero calls Thorius was really quite another person. However that may be, the law would benefit the rich, because the rich would be owners of the land. Certain provisions of it were directly meant to prevent opposition in the country. For if many of the poor farmers would grumble at being ousted from their land, the land which had been specially assigned to Latin towns, and of which Tiberius Gracchus had threatened to dispossess them, was left in the same state as before his legislation; that is to say, the Senate did not give the occupiers an indefeasible title, but it did not meddle with them. Moreover, it amply indemnified the Socii and Latini who had surrendered land for the colonies of Caius, while some compensation was given to poor farmers by a clause, that in future a man might only graze ten large and fifty smaller beasts on the pastures of what still remained public land. By this law the jurisdiction over land which had been assigned by the triumvirs was given to the consuls, censors, and praetors, the jurisdiction over cases in which disputes with the publicani required settlement being granted to the consuls, praetors, and, as such cases would occur chiefly in the provinces which were mostly under propraetors, to propraetors also.

[Pernicious results of the reaction.] The results of this reactionary legislation are partly summed up by Appian, when he attributes to it a dearth of citizens, soldiers, and revenue. To our eyes its effects are clearer still. Slave labour and slave-discontent, 'latifundia,' decrease of population, depreciation of the land, received a fresh impetus, and the triumphant optimates pushed the State step by step further down the road to ruin. For the end for which they struggled was not the good of Italy, much less of the world, but the supremacy of Rome in Italy, and of themselves in Rome. Wealth and office were shared by an ever narrowing circle. Ten years after the passing of the Baebian law, it was said that among all the citizens there were only 2,000 wealthy families. And between the years 123 and 109 B.C. four sons and probably two nephews of Quintus Metellus gained the consulship, five of the six gained triumphs, and one was censor, while he himself had filled all the highest offices of the State. Thus, as Sallust says, the nobles passed on the chief dignities from hand to hand.

There must have been many of the Gracchan party, now left without a head, who burned for deliverance from such despicable masters. But they were for the time disorganized and cowed. [Caius Marius.] There was one man whom Scipio Aemilianus was said to have pointed out in the Numantine war as capable, if he himself died, of taking his place; and the rough soldier had already come forward as a politician, on the one hand checking the optimates by protecting the secrecy and efficiency of the ballot, and on the other defying the mob by opposing a distribution of corn; but for the present no one could tell how far he would or could go, and though he had already been made praetor, the Metelli could as yet afford to despise him. The death of Caius prolonged the Senate's misrule for twenty years. Twenty years of shame at home and abroad—the turpitude of the Jugurthine war—a second and more stubborn slave revolt in Sicily—the apparition of the Northern hordes inflicting disaster after disaster upon the Roman armies, which in 105 B.C. culminated in another and more appalling Cannae—these things had yet to come about before the cup of the Senate's infamy was full, and before those who had drawn the sword against the Gracchi perished by the sword of Marius, impotent, unpitied, and despised.
* * * * *

CHAPTER IV.THE JUGURTHINE WAR.

Attalus III., the last of that supple dynasty which had managed to thrive on the jealous and often treacherous patronage of Rome, left his dominions at his death to the Republic. He had begun his reign by massacring all his father's friends and their families, and ended it as an amateur gardener and dilettante modeller in wax; so perhaps the malice of insanity had something to do with the bequest, if indeed it was not a forgery. Aristonicus, a natural son of a previous king, Eumenes II., set it at naught and aspired to the throne.

[Aristonicus usurps the kingdom of Pergamus.] Attalus died in 133, the year of the tribunate of Tiberius Gracchus, when Scipio was besieging Numantia, and the first slave revolt was raging in Sicily. The Romans had their hands full, and Aristonicus might have so established himself as to give them trouble, had not some of the Asiatic cities headed by Ephesus, and aided by the kings of Cappadocia and Bithynia, opposed him. He seized Leucae (the modern Lefke) and was expelled by the Ephesians. But when the Senate found time to send commissioners, he was already in possession of Thyatira, Apollonia, Myndus, Colophon, and Samos. Blossius, the friend of Gracchus, had come to him, and the civil strife at Rome must have raised his hopes.

[Conduct of Crassus, illustrating Roman rule in the province.] But in the year 131 P. Licinius Crassus Mucianus, the father-in-law of Caius Gracchus, was consul, and was sent to Asia. He was Pontifex Maximus, rich, high-born, eloquent, and of great legal knowledge; and from his intimacy with the Gracchi and Scipio he must have been an unusually favourable specimen of the aristocrat of the day. And this is what he did in Asia. He was going to besiege Leucae, and having seen two pieces of timber at Elaea, sent for the larger of them to make a battering ram. The builder, who was the chief magistrate of the town, sent him the smaller piece as being the most suitable, and Crassus had him stripped and scourged. Next year he was surprised by the enemy near Leucae. Apparently he could have got off if he had not been laden with his collections in Asia, to procure which he had intrigued to prevent his colleague Flaccus getting that province. Unable to escape, he provoked his captor to kill him by thrusting a stick into his eye. His death was a striking comment on the Senate's government. Cruelty and culture, personal bravery and. incompetence—such an alloy was now the best metal which its most respectable representatives could supply.

[End of Aristonicus and settlement of the kingdom.] Aristonicus was now the more formidable because he had roused the slaves, among whom the spirit of revolt, in sympathy with the rest of their kind throughout the Roman world, was then working. But in the year 130 M. Perperna surprised him, and carried him to Rome. Blossius committed suicide. The pretender was strangled in prison. Part of his territory was given to the kings who had helped the consul, one of whom was the father of the great Mithridates. Phrygia was the share assigned to him; but the Senate took it back from his successor, saying that the consul Aquillius had been bribed to give it. The consul may have been base or the Senate mean, or, what is more probable, the baseness of the one was used as a welcome plea by the other's meanness. The European part was added to the province of Macedonia. The Lycian confederacy received Telmissus. The rest was formed into a province, which was called Asia—the name being at once an incentive to and a nucleus for future annexation. Such a nucleus they already possessed in the province of Africa, and there also war was kindled by the ambition of a bastard.

[Jugurtha.] Jugurtha was the illegitimate son of Mastanabal, Micipsa's brother. He had served at Numantia under Scipio, along with his future conqueror Marius. There he had begun to intrigue with influential Romans for the succession to the Numidian kingdom, and had been rebuked by Scipio, who told him he should cultivate the friendship, not of individual Romans, but of the State. But in Jugurtha's heart a noble sentiment found no echo. Brave, treacherous, restless, an able commander, a crafty politician, adroit in discerning and profiting by other men's bad qualities, wading to the throne through the blood of three kinsmen, he in some respects resembles Shakspeare's Richard III.,—his 'prime of manhood daring, bold, and venturous,' his 'age confirmed, proud, subtle, sly, and bloody.' [Micipsa's will.] Micipsa had shared the kingdom with his two brothers, who died before him; and as this, which was Scipio's arrangement, had not worked badly in his own case, he in his turn left his kingdom between Adherbal, Hiempsal, and Jugurtha. Adherbal was weak and pusillanimous, Hiempsal hot-tempered and rash. Jugurtha, ten or fifteen years older than either, was the favourite of the nation, his handsome, martial figure and his reputation as a soldier according with the notions of a race of riders as to what a king should be. Hiempsal soon provoked him by refusing to yield the place of honour to him at their first meeting; and when Jugurtha said that Micipsa's acts during the last five years of his life should be held as null because of his impaired faculties, Hiempsal retorted that he agreed with him, for it was within three years that he had adopted Jugurtha. [Jugurtha gets rid of Hiempsal.] Hiempsal went to a town called Thirmida, to the house of a man who had been in Jugurtha's service. This man Jugurtha bribed to procure a model of the town keys, which were taken to Hiempsal each evening. Then his men, getting into Thirmida one night, cut off Hiempsal's head and took it to their master. He then proceeded to seize town after town; all the best warriors rallied to his standard, and in a pitched battle he defeated Adherbal, who fled to Rome, whither he had previously sent ambassadors imploring aid. Jugurtha also sent envoys with plenty of money, to be given first to his old comrades, and then to men likely to be useful. At once the indignation which the wrongs of the brothers had roused at Rome cooled down. [M. Aemilius Scaurus.] But M. Aemilius Scaurus, the chief of the aristocracy, seems to have been bidding for a higher price than was at first offered him, and by his influence ten commissioners were appointed to divide the kingdom. Scaurus had in his youth thought of becoming a money-lender, a trade in which he would certainly have excelled; and he may very likely have hoped to make something out of the commission, as the exemplary Opimius, murderer of Caius Gracchus, did. [Jugurtha bribes the commissioners.] This man, whom Cicero extols as a most excellent citizen, had opposed Jugurtha at Rome but being in consequence treated by the king in Numidia with marked deference, joined the majority of his colleagues in swallowing the bribes offered to them. So Adherbal received the eastern half which, though it contained the capital Cirta and better harbours and towns, consisted mostly of barren sand, while the more fertile portion was assigned to his rival.

[Jugurtha assails Adherbal, who appeals to the Senate.] This took place in the year 117 B.C. Scarcely had the commissioners left the province when the successful villain again took up arms. Adherbal, after much long-suffering and sending a complaint to Rome, was driven to do the same in self-defence. But he was defeated between Cirta and the sea, and would have been taken in Cirta had not the colony of Italians resident there beaten off the horsemen in pursuit. [A second commission, hoaxed or bribed by Jugurtha.] Meanwhile Adherbal's message had reached Rome, and the Senate, with its high sense of responsibility, sent ten young men to Numidia as adjudicators. Perhaps, indeed, it was not mere carelessness which sent these young hopefuls to the best school of bribery in the world. They were bidden to insist simply on the war ceasing, and the two kings settling their disputes by law. And yet the news of the battle and the siege of Cirta had reached Rome. Jugurtha came to them, and said that his merits had won Scipio's approval, and that, conscious of right, he could not submit to wrong; he then gravely charged Adherbal with plotting against his life, and promised to send ambassadors to Rome. Then the ten young men without even seeing Adherbal, left Africa, not we may conjecture so lightly laden as they came there.

The town of Cirta stood on the promontory of a peninsula formed by a loop of the river Ampsaga, and was almost impregnable. Modern writers represent it as a square spur, thrust out into a gorge which runs between two mountain-ranges, this gorge being spanned by a bridge at one corner of the square. The town, now known as Constantina, and distant 48 miles from the sea and 200 from Algiers, has been described as occupying a bold and commanding situation on a steep, rocky hill, with the river Rummel flowing on three sides of its base, the country around being a high terrace between the chains of the maritime and central Atlas. [Adherbal blockaded in Cirta.] Such being the strength of the place, Jugurtha could only hope to reduce it by blockade, and it was only after four months that two of Adherbal's men got out and carried a piteous appeal from their master to the Senate, adjuring them, not indeed to give him back his kingdom, but to save his life. [A third commission.] Some of the Senate were for sending an army to Africa at once, but in those days honest men were always in the minority, and three commissioners were sent instead—Scaurus, the man who had so lively an appreciation of his own value, at their head. [Jugurtha is admonished by it.] Jugurtha, after a desperate attempt to storm Cirta before they arrived, came to them at Utica, where he was admonished at great length. Then this precious trio left Africa, as the ten young men had done; and the surrender of Cirta followed, either because despair led its defenders to hope that submission, as it would save the enemy trouble, might conciliate him, or perhaps because water or food ran short. [Cirta taken and Adherbal murdered.] Jugurtha immediately tortured Adherbal to death, and put every Numidian and Italian in the place to the sword.

[Genuine indignation at Rome.] Then at last a thrill of genuine anger went through Rome. The honour of the State had been sorely wounded, but gold had been thus far a pleasant salve. Now, however, the equites were touched in their hearts at the fate probably of some of their own kinsmen, and almost certainly in an even more sensitive part—their purses. For no doubt there were commercial relations between the Italian community at Cirta and the Roman merchants, and here their gains were confiscated at one stroke by a savage. The senators, on the other hand, who had taken Numidian money, tried to quash discussion, and would have succeeded if the tribune, Caius Memmius, had not overawed them by his harangues. [War declared. Bestia sails to Africa.] Fresh envoys, who had been sent by Jugurtha with a fresh bribery fund, were ordered to leave Italy in ten days; and Bestia sailed for Africa, taking with him as his second in command Scaurus, who felt, no doubt, that a patriot was at last rewarded. [Jugurtha bribes the generals.] There was some fighting, and then the money from which Roman virtue had shrunk in Italy could be resisted no longer. The itching palm of Scaurus was at length filled as full as he thought mere decency demanded. Bestia was also gratified, Jugurtha's submission was accepted, hostilities ceased, and the consul sailed home to superintend the next year's elections. [Harangues of the tribune Memmius.] But Memmius, justly incensed, now took a bolder tone. We cannot tell how far Sallust reports what he really said, or how far he drew on his own invention. But if he has given us Memmius's own words, they must have rung in the ears of many an honest Roman like the trumpet-notes of that still more eloquent tribune whose body, ten years before, had been hurled into the Tiber. For he cast in the teeth of his audience their pusillanimity in suffering their champions to be murdered, and allowing so worthless a crew to lord it over them. It had been shameful enough that they had witnessed in silence the plunder of the treasury, the monopoly of all high office, and kings and free states cringing to a handful of nobles; but now a worse thing had been done, and the honour of the Republic trafficked away. And the men who had done this felt neither shame nor sorrow, but strutted about with a parade of triumphs, consulships, and priesthoods, as if they were men of honour and not thieves. After these and similar home-thrusts, he called upon the people to insist on Jugurtha being brought to Rome, for so they would test the reality of his surrender. The tribune's eloquence prevailed. The praetor Cassius was sent to bring Jugurtha under a promise of safe-conduct. Jugurtha hesitated. Bestia's officers were treading in their general's steps, taking bribes, selling as slaves the Numidians who had deserted to them, and pillaging the country. Jugurtha was fast becoming the national hero instead of the chief of a faction, and might have even then dreamt of defying Rome. However, he yielded and, as it was not in his nature to do things by halves, came in the mean dress which was assumed to excite compassion. He did more. This was the year of the so-called Thorian law. [Jugurtha comes to Rome, and bribes the tribune Baebius.] Caius Baebius, who may have been the author of that law, was tribune, and not of the stamp of Memmius. He took Jugurtha's bribes, and when the king was being cross-questioned by Memmius, interposed his veto, and forbade him to reply. Thus once again, though the people were furious, the old plan seemed to be working well.

[Murder of Massiva.] But now a cousin of the king, named Massiva, a grandson of Masinissa, at the instigation of the consul Albinus, claimed the Numidian crown. In the present state of parties he was sure of support, so Jugurtha had recourse to the second weapon which he always used when the first was useless. He had him assassinated by his adherent Bomilcar, and assisted the latter to escape from Italy. At last his savage audacity had overstepped even the forbearance of the rogues in his pay. [Jugurtha expelled from Rome.] He was ordered to leave Rome, and, as he went, uttered the famous epigram, 'A city for sale, and when the first buyer comes, doomed to ruin!' [Futile campaign of Albinus.] It is possible that Spurius Albinus, who was next sent against him, was playing the game of Scaurus and Bestia over again; for he effected nothing in his campaign in 110. Nor does his brother's rashness exonerate him. Left as propraetor in charge of the army, this man, in January 109, determined to try and carry off Jugurtha's treasures by a coup de main. To do this he marched against Suthul, where the treasures were kept, at a season when the heavy rains turn the land into water. [Jugurtha overthrows Aulus Albinus.] Jugurtha retreated

into the interior, enticing Aulus Albinus by hopes of coming to terms, and meanwhile tampering with his officers. Then, on a dark night, he surrounded the army. The traitors whom he had bribed deserted their posts. The soldiers threw away their arms, and next day Jugurtha forced Aulus to agree to go under the yoke, to make peace, and, perhaps, in mockery of the Senate's treatment of the Numidian envoys, to leave Numidia in ten days. Of course the Senate would not acknowledge the treaty. Nor did they even go through the farce of surrendering the man who had made it. The chivalry of the era of Regulus would have seemed quixotic to cynics like Scaurus. The other Albinus, hastening to Africa, found the troops mutinous, and could effect nothing. Another tribune now stepped forward to impeach all, whether soldiers or civilians, who had assisted Jugurtha to the prejudice of the State. In spite of the aid of the rich Latins, who had just been gratified by the remission of the vectigal, the senators were beaten and the bill passed. Triumvirs were appointed to investigate the matter; but one of them was Scaurus, sure to float most buoyantly where the scum of scoundrelism was thickest. [Banishment of Romans who had taken Jugurtha's bribes.] The judices were equites, and among those condemned were Bestia, Sp. Albinus, Opimius, and Caius Cato, the grandson of Cato the censor. Opimius died at Dyrrhachium, a poor man; and probably no harder punishment could have befallen him.
The history of the Jugurthine war has been thus far related at greater length than the space at command would warrant if it was merely a history of military details. But it is a striking commentary on the politics of the time and the vices of the government. The state of society could not be more succinctly summed up than in the words with which Jugurtha quitted Rome. What was it which made the nobles so greedy of money as to be lost to all shame in hunting for it? A speech supposed to have been delivered that very year partly answers the question: 'Gourmands say that a meal is not all that it ought to be unless, precisely when you are relishing most what you are eating, your plate is removed and another, and better, and richer one is put in its place. Your exquisite, who makes extravagance and fastidiousness pass for wit, calls that the "bloom of a meal." "The only bird," says he, "which you should eat whole is the becafico. Of every other bird, wild or tame, nothing, unless your host be a mean fellow, but the hinder parts will be served, and enough of them to satisfy everybody. People who eat the fore parts have no palate." If luxury goes on at this rate there will soon be nothing left but for them to have their meats nibbled at for them by some one else, to save them the toil of eating. Already the couches of some men are decorated more lavishly with silver and purple and gold than those of the immortal gods.'
If the war up to this stage had revealed the hopeless depravity of the senatorial government, its subsequent course revealed what shape the revolution about to engulf that government would assume. The consulship of Marius, won in spite of Metellus, signified really the fall of the Republic and the rise of monarchy, while the rivalry of Marius and Sulla showed that supreme authority would be competed for, not in the forum but the camp. The law of Manilius necessitated an earnest prosecution of the war. [Metellus appointed to the command against Jugurtha. His character.] Quintus Caecilius Metellus was elected consul for the year 109, and received Numidia as his province. He was a stern, proud man; but if in his childish hauteur he had a double portion of the foible of his order, he was free from many of its vices. He set to work at once to rediscipline the army; and his punishment of deserters, abominable in itself, was no doubt an effective warning that the new general was not a man with whom it was safe to trifle. The Romans were never gentle to the deserter unless he deserted to them. They threw him to wild beasts, or cut off his hands. Metellus did more. He buried 3,000 men to their waists, made the soldiers use them as targets, and finally burned them.

[Battle on the Muthul.] Jugurtha was alarmed, and sent to offer terms, asking only a guarantee for his life. Metellus returned evasive answers, and secretly intrigued with the messengers for the surrender or assassination of the king. But though assassination had become one of the recognised weapons of a Roman noble, Metellus was a novice in the art by the side of Jugurtha, who determined to die hard now he was at bay. The Romans had to cross a range of mountains, after which they descended into a plain through which the river Muthul (probably a branch of the modern Mejerda) ran eighteen miles off. Between them and the river was hilly ground— probably a spur from the range. On this hilly ground the king posted Bomilcar, with the infantry and elephants. He himself, with the best of the foot and the cavalry, waited nearer the mountains. Metellus saw the snare, but was obliged to get water, and in making for the river was surrounded. But the new discipline told. Though isolated, each Roman division fought bravely. Metellus and Marius carried the hills. Rufus dispersed the picked infantry, and killed or captured all the elephants. Jugurtha's plan was masterly, but it had failed. [Jugurtha keeps up a guerilla warfare.] His army dispersed, as such armies do upon defeat, and he was reduced to carrying on a guerilla warfare, spoiling the springs where Metellus was marching, and cutting off stragglers. Metellus split his army into two columns; Marius commanded one and he the other, and so they marched, ravaging the country and capturing the towns, ready to form a junction whenever it was necessary. At last they came to Zama; and, while Metellus was attempting to storm the town, Jugurtha surprised his camp. Though beaten off in this assault he attacked the Romans again next day, and Metellus was obliged to give up his enterprise. [Metellus tampers with Bomilcar.] After garrisoning the towns which he had taken, he went into winter quarters, probably at Utica, where he proceeded to tamper with Bomilcar. That traitor urged Jugurtha to surrender, and the king gave up his elephants, the deserters, and a large sum of money. But when it came to giving up himself his heart failed him, and, having discovered Bomilcar's treachery, he slew him, and once more resolved to fight.

[Marius stands for the consulship, 107 B.C.] The preceding military operations are supposed to have taken place in the year 108 B.C. Marius went to Rome to stand for the consulship, and while he was away, in 107, Metellus retained the command. Jugurtha's cause even now was not hopeless. The Numidians adored him, and were smarting under the Roman devastations. [Revolt of Vaga.] The chief town occupied by the Romans, Vaga—the modern Baja—revolted in the winter, and the commander, Turpilius, a Latin, rightly or wrongly was executed by Metellus for collusion with the enemy. But Metellus was eager to end the war, and pressed the king hard. Jugurtha lost another battle, and fled to Thala; but Metellus marched fifty miles across the desert, and forced him to flee by night out of the town, which was taken after a siege of forty days. But now a new enemy confronted the Romans. [Bocchus joins Jugurtha.] Bocchus, king of Mauretania, formed an alliance with his son-in-law, Jugurtha, and was induced by him to march against Cirta, which was in the possession of the Romans. About the same time Metellus heard that Marius was coming to supersede him. The proud man shed tears of rage, and would not move further for fear of hazarding his own reputation, or lessening the difficulties of his successor.

[Marius succeeds to the command.] The African war now promised hard work and little glory or profit to the soldiers, and Jugurtha's bribing days were over. Hence it was hard to recruit the legions, and Marius took men from the Proletarii and Capite Censi, classes usually exempt from service. With these troops, who would be more easily satisfied and more manageable, he filled up the gaps in the legions in Africa, and set to work, as Metellus had done, taking towns and forts and plundering the country. Bocchus had separated from Jugurtha, for they hoped that the

Romans having two foes to chase would be the more easily harassed. But Marius was always on his guard, and beat, though he could never capture, Jugurtha whenever he came across him. [Capture of Capsa.] There is an oasis in the south of Tunis, and a town, Gafsa, in it, which in those days was called Capsa. This town Marius captured after a laborious march of nine or ten days, and, though the inhabitants surrendered, he ruthlessly massacred every adult Numidian in it, and sold the rest as slaves. One other exploit of his is told by Sallust, but with such blunders of geography as render identification of the place impossible. Carrying fire and sword through the land, Marius reached a fort in which the king's treasures were. It stood on a precipice, which was considered inaccessible on all sides but one. For many days he strove in vain to gain the walls by this road, and only an accident saved him from failure in the end. A Ligurian in the army, while gathering snails, unconsciously got nearly to the top of the hill. Finding this out he clambered further and got a full view of the town. [Capture of another stronghold.] Next day Marius sent ten men with horns and trumpets and the Ligurian as guide, while he himself assailed the town by the road. As soon as they were at the top he ordered an assault on the walls. The men marched up with their shields locked over their heads, and at the same moment the Roman trumpets were heard at the side of the town over the precipice. The Numidians fled and the fort was won. [Marius marches for Cirta.] Here, wherever the place was, Marius was joined by Sulla with some cavalry; and having gained his end, he marched eastward towards Cirta, intending to winter his men in the maritime towns. [Attempts of Jugurtha to surprise his march.] But the Numidian king had nerved himself for one last desperate effort. By the promise of a third of his kingdom he bribed Bocchus to join him, and one night at dusk surprised the retiring army. Only discipline saved it. Like the English at Inkermann, the Romans fought in small detached groups, till Marius was able to concentrate his men on a hill, while Sulla by his orders occupied another hard by. The barbarians surrounded them and kept up a revel all night, deeming their prey secure. But at dawn Marius bade the horns strike up, and with a shout the soldiers charged down and dispersed the enemy with ease. Then the march went on till they were near Cirta. Again Jugurtha attempted to cut off the retreat. Volux, son of Bocchus, had brought him some fresh infantry. While the cavalry engaged Sulla, Bocchus led these men round to attack the rear. Jugurtha, who was fighting against Masinissa in the front, rode also to the rear, and, holding up a bloody head, cried out that he had slain Marius. The Romans began to give way, when Sulla, like Cromwell at Marston Moor, having done his own work charged the troops of Bocchus on the flank. Still Jugurtha fought on, and fled only when all around him were slain. The result of this battle was that Bocchus became anxious to come to terms. Sulla was sent to arrange them. But Bocchus hated the Romans, while he feared them; and fresh solicitations from Jugurtha made him again waver. [Negotiations of Bocchus with Rome.] Soon afterwards, by permission of Marius, he sent an embassy to Rome. The Senate replied that they excused his past errors, and that he should have the friendship and alliance of Rome when he had earned it. Then ensued intrigue upon intrigue. [Sulla persuades Bocchus to betray Jugurtha.] Sulla daringly visited Bocchus, and after some days' hesitation, during which Sulla pressed him to betray Jugurtha, and Jugurtha pressed him to betray Sulla, the Moorish king at last decided on which side his interests lay. The Roman devised a trap. The arch-traitor was ensnared, and was carried in chains to Rome, where he was led in his royal robes by the triumphal car of Marius, and, it is said, lost his senses as he walked along. One wonders with what relish Scaurus and his tribe, after gazing at the spectacle, sat down to their becaficoes that day. Then he was thrust into prison, and as they hasted to strip him, some tore the clothes off his back, while others in wrenching out his earrings pulled off the tips of his ears with them. And so he was thrust down naked into the Tullianum. 'Hercules, what a cold bath!' he cried, with the wild smile of idiocy, as they cast him in. [Death of Jugurtha.] For six days he endured the torments of starvation, and then died. [Division of the Numidian kingdom.] The most westerly portion of his kingdom, corresponding to the modern province of Algiers, was given to Bocchus, the rest of it to Gauda, Jugurtha's half-brother. The Romans did not care to turn into a province a country of which the frontiers were so hard to guard. But they received some Gaetulian tribes in the interior into free alliance, so that they had plenty of opportunities for meddling if they wished to do so.

* * * * *

CHAPTER V. THE CIMBRI AND TEUTONES.

The Jugurthine war ended in 105 B.C. In one way it had been of real service to Rome. A terrible crisis was at hand, and this war had given her both soldiers and a general worthy of the name. Before, however, the story of the struggle with the Cimbri is told, something must be said about what had been going on at Rome, about the man who had now most influence there, and about his rivals. The great social struggle had recommenced. The personal rivalry between Marius and Sulla had begun before the Cimbric war. During that war men held as it were their breath in terror, but nevertheless it was as if only an interlude in that deadly civil strife, for which each of the contending parties was already arrayed. C. Marius was now fifty years old. Cato, the censor, was of opinion that no man can endure so much as he who has turned the soil and reaped the harvest. Marius was such a man. His family were clients of the Herennii. His father was a day-labourer of Cereatae, called today Casamare, after his illustrious son, and he himself served in the ranks in Spain. [Previous career and present position of Marius.] Soon made an officer, he won Scipio's favour as a brave, frugal, incorruptible, and trusty soldier, who never quarrelled with his general's orders, even when they ran as counter to his own inclinations as the expulsion of all soothsayers from the camp before Numantia. On coming home he was lucky enough to marry the aunt of Julius Caesar, whose high birth and wealth opened the door to State honours, which to a man of his origin was at this time otherwise virtually closed. In 119 B.C. he was tribune, and had by the measures previously noticed won the reputation of an upright and patriotic politician, who would truckle neither to the nobles nor the mob. From this time, however, the feud with the Metelli began; for he ordered L. Caecilius Metellus, the consul, to be cast into prison for resisting his ballot-law, though, as the Senate yielded, the order was not carried into effect. In 115 he gained the praetorship, and an absurd charge of bribery trumped up against him indicated a rising disposition among the nobles to snub the aspiring plebeian. He was propraetor in Spain the next year, and showed his usual vigour there in putting down brigandage. With the soldiers he was as popular as Ney was with Napoleon's armies, for he was one of them, rough-spoken as they were, fond of a cup of wine, and never scorning to share their toils. While he was with Metellus at Utica, a soothsayer prophesied that the gods had great things in store for him, and he asked Metellus for leave to go to Rome and stand for the consulship. Metellus replied that when his own son stood for it it would be time enough for Marius. The man at whom he sneered resented sneers. There is evidence that the simple nature of the rough soldier was becoming already spoiled by constant success. He was burning with ambition, and would ascribe the favours of heaven to his own merits. He at once set to work to undermine the credit of his commander with the army, the Roman merchants, and Gauda, saying that he himself would soon bring the war to an end if he were general. Metellus can hardly have been a popular man anywhere, and his strictness must have made him many enemies. Thus he scornfully refused Gauda a seat at his side, and an escort of Roman horse. Gauda and the rest wrote to Rome, urging that Marius should have the army. Metellus with the worst grace let him go just twelve days before the election. But the favourite of the gods had a fair wind, and travelled night and day. The artisans of the city and the country class from which he sprang thronged to hear him abuse Metellus, and boast how soon he would capture or kill Jugurtha, and he was triumphantly elected consul for the year 107.

How his after achievements turned his head we shall see. Already there were drops of bitterness in the sweet cup of success. It was Metellus who was called Numidicus, not he, and it was Sulla whose dare-devil knavery had entrapped the king. The substantial work had been done by the former. The coup de théâtre which completed it revealed the latter as a rival. Marius fumed at the credit gained by these aristocrats; and when Bocchus dedicated on the Capitol a representation of Sulla receiving Jugurtha's surrender, he could not conceal his wrath. [L. Cornelius Sulla.] In Sulla he perhaps already recognised by instinct one who would outrival him in the end. He was the very antipodes of Marius in everything except bravery and good generalship, and faith in his star. He was an aristocrat. He was dissolute. He was an admirer of Hellenic literature. War was not his all in all as a profession. If he had a lion's courage, the fox in him was even more to be feared. He, like Marius, owed his rise partly to a woman, but, characteristically, to a mistress, not a wife, who helped him as Charles II.'s sultana helped the young Churchill. If the boorish nature of the one degenerated with age into bloodthirsty brutality, the other was from the first cynically destitute of feeling. He would send men to death with a jest, and the cold-blooded, calculating, remorseless infamy of his entire career excites a repulsion which we feel for no other great figure in history, not even for the first Napoleon. Sulla's whole soul must have recoiled from the coarse manners of the man under whom he first won distinction, and, while he scorned his motives, he must, as he saw him gradually floundering into villainy, have felt the serene superiority of a natural genius for vice. But at present it was not his game to show his animosity. Though Marius had given fresh umbrage to the optimates by coming from his triumph (Jan. 1, 104 B.C.) into the Senate wearing his triumphal robes, with the people he was the hero of the hour, and when the storm in the North broke, it was the safest course for Sulla to follow the fortunes of his old commander, who in his turn could not dispense with so able a subordinate.

[Frontier wars of Rome previous to the Cimbric invasion.] The Romans were constantly at war on the frontiers. Besides the natural quarrels which would arise between them and lawless barbarians, it was the interest of their generals to make small wars in order to gain sounding names and triumphs. Such wars, however, by no means always ended in Roman victories; and while in the last thirty years of the second century before the Christian era there were many wars, there were also many defeats. [The Iapydes.] Sempronius Tuditanus had a triumph for victories over the Iapydes, an Illyrian nation; but he was first beaten by them. [The Salyes.] In 125 the Salyes, a Ligurian people, who stretched from Marseilles westwards to the Rhone and northwards to the Durance, attacked Marseilles. Flaccus went to its aid, and triumphed over the Salyes in 123. [The Balearic Islands.] Quintus Caecilius Metellus subdued the Balearic Islands in the same year, and relieved Spain from the descents of pirates, who either lived in those islands or used them as a rendezvous. The Salyes again gave trouble in 122, and Calvinus took their capital, which was most probably the modern Aix, establishing there the colony of Aquae Sextiae. This colony was the point d'appui for further conquests. The most powerful nations of Gaul were the Aedui and Arverni, whose territory was separated by the Elaver, the modern Allier. The Arverni were rivals of the Aedui and friends of the Allobroges, a tribe in the same latitude, but on the east of the Rhone. The Romans made an alliance with the Aedui, and the proconsul Domitius Ahenobarbus, in 122 or 121 B.C., charged the Allobroges with violating

Aeduan territory, and with harbouring the king of the Salyes. [The Allobroges.] The Allobroges were helped by the Arverni, and Domitius defeated their united forces near Avignon, with the loss of 20,000 men. Fabius succeeded Domitius, and marched northwards across the Isara. [The Arverni.] Near its junction with the Rhone, on August 8, 121, he defeated with tremendous carnage the Arverni who had crossed to help the Allobroges. [Defeat of the Arverni, B.C. 121.] The number of the slain amounted, it is said, to 120,000 or 150,000. The king of the Arverni was caught and sent to Rome, and the Allobroges became Roman subjects. It was the year of the death of Caius Gracchus, of the famous vintage, and of a great eruption of Mount Etna. [The Staeni.] In 118 B.C. M. Marcius Rex annihilated the Staeni, probably a Ligurian tribe of the Maritime Alps, who were in the line of the Roman approach to South Gaul, and for this success he gained a triumph. In the same year it was resolved, in spite of the opposition of the Senate, to colonise Narbo, which was the key to the valley of the Garonne, and was on the route to the province of Tarraconensis. Thus was established the province named from the time of Augustus the Narbonensis, embracing the country between the Cevennes and the Alps, as far north-east as Geneva; and a road, called Via Domitia, was laid down from the Rhone to the Pyrenees. [The Dalmatae.] In 117 B.C. L. Caecilius Metellus triumphed over the Illyrian Dalmatae whom he had attacked without cause, or never attacked at all, as it was said, for which he was surnamed Dalmaticus. [The Karni.] In 115 M. Aemilius Scaurus, whose name we have met with before, triumphed over the Karni, a tribe to the north of the Adriatic. C. Porcius Cato, consul in 114, was not so lucky. [The Scordisci.] He lost his army in defending the Macedonian frontier against a tribe of Gauls called Scordisci, who were in their turn defeated by M. Livius Drusus in 112, and M. Minucius Rufus in 109 B.C. The year between their first victory and first defeat was remarkable, not, indeed, because one Metellus triumphed for what he had done in Sardinia, and another for what he had done in Thrace; but in that year the Cimbri came in collision with Rome. [First collision with Cimbri.] Cn. Papirius Carbo, the consul, was sent against them as they had crossed or were expected to cross the Roman frontiers. Some were in Noricum, and to them he sent to say that they were invading a people who were the friends of Rome. They agreed to evacuate the country; but Carbo treacherously attacked them, and was disgracefully beaten at a place called Noreia. [Defeat of Silanus.] Four years later, in the year 109, M. Junius Silanus, colleague of Marius, met the same barbarians, who had now crossed the Rhine, in the new province of South Gaul, and was in his turn defeated.

[The Cimbri rouse the Helvetii.] The movements of the Cimbri made the Helvetii restless. [Defeat of Longinus.] One of their clans, the Tiguroni, which dwelt between the Jura, the Rhone, and the lake of Geneva, defeated and slew the consul Longinus in 107 B.C., and forced his lieutenant, Popillius Laenas, to go under the yoke. Tolosa thereupon rose against the Romans, and put the troops which garrisoned it in chains. By treachery Q. Servilius Caepio recovered the town, and sent off its treasures to Marseilles. [The gold of Tolosa.] The ill-gotten gold, however, was seized on the way by robbers, whom Caepio himself was accused of employing. His name was destined, however, to be linked with a great disaster as well as a thievish trick. The Cimbri, who had hitherto petitioned the Romans for lands to settle on, were now meditating a raid into Italy. On the left bank of the Rhone, in 105, they overthrew M. Aurelius Scaurus, whom they took prisoner and put to death. Cnaeus Mallius Maximus commanded the main force on that side of the river, and he told Caepio, who as consul was in command on the right bank, to cross and effect a junction. But Caepio was as wilful as Minucius had shown himself towards another Maximus in the Second Punic War. When his superior began to negotiate with the Cimbri, he thought it was a device to rob him of the honour of conquering them, and in his irritation rashly provoked a battle, in which he was beaten and lost his camp. [Defeat of Caepio and Maximus.] The place of his defeat his camp is not known. Maximus was also defeated, and the Romans were reported to have lost 80,000 men and 20,000 camp followers. There was terrible dismay at Rome. The Gaul seemed again to be at its gates. [Consternation at Rome. Marius elected consul for 104.] The time of mourning for the dead was abridged. Every man fit for service had to swear not to leave Italy, and the captains in Italian ports took an oath not to receive any such man on board. Marius also was elected consul for 104.

[The Cimbri move off towards Spain.] But fortune helped the Romans more than all these precautions. The Cimbri, after wilfully destroying every vestige of the spoils they had taken, in fulfilment, probably, of some vow, wandered westward on a plundering raid towards the Pyrenees, the road thither having been lately provided, as it were, for them by Domitius. [Beaten back by Celtiberi, they are joined by the Teutones in South Gaul.] In the Celtiberi they met with foes who sold too dearly the little they had to lose, and again they surged back into South Gaul, where they were joined by the Teutones, and once more threatened Italy. [How the Romans had been occupied meanwhile.] But meantime the generals of the Republic had not been idle. Rutilius Rufus, the old comrade of Marius, had been diligently drilling troops, having engaged gladiators to teach them fencing. Probably Marius was engaged in the same work at the beginning of 104, and then went to South Gaul, where, as we hear of Sulla capturing the king of the Tectosages, he was no doubt collecting supplies and men, and suppressing all disaffection in the province. He also cut a canal from the Rhone, about a mile above its mouth, to a lake supposed to be now the Étang de l'Estouma; for alluvial deposits had made access to the river difficult, and he wanted the Rhone as a highway for his troops and commissariat. [Marius consul in 103 and 102 B.C.] In 103 he was made consul for the third time, and again in 102. And now he was ready to meet the invaders.

[Nationality of the Cimbri.] Who these invaders were has been a matter of hot dispute. Were they Celts? Were they Teutons? Did they come from the Baltic shores, or the shores of the Sea of Azof; or were they the Homeric Cimmerii who dwelt between the Dnieper and the Don? Or did their name indicate their personal qualities, and not their previous habitation? The following seems the most probable conjecture. In the great plain which runs along the Atlantic and the southern shore of the Baltic, from the Pyrenees to the Volga, there had been in pre-historic times a movement constantly going on among the barbarous inhabitants like the ebb and flow of a great sea. The Celts had reached Spain and Italy on the south, and Germany and the Danube on the east. Then, making the Rhine their frontier, they had settled down into semi-civilised life. Now the Teutonic tribes were in their turn going through the same process of flux and reflux; and impelled probably at this time by some invasion of other tribes, or possibly, as Strabo says, by some great inundation of the sea, these invading nations, for they were not armies but whole nations, came roaming southwards in search of a new home. Celts there were among them, for the Helvetii had joined them, and therefore Helvetic chiefs. But the names still exist in modern Denmark and near the Baltic. Caesar did not think they were Celts. The light hair and blue eyes of the warriors, and the hair of old age on the heads of children, which excited the astonishment of the Romans, are not Celtic characteristics. We may therefore set them down as Teutonic by race. The name Cimbri is probably derived from some word of their own, Kaemper, meaning champions or spoilers, and their last emigration was from the country between the Rhine, the Danube, and the Baltic. They were a tall, fierce race, who fought with great swords and narrow shields, and wore copper helmets and mail. [Their mode of fighting, etc.] The men in their front ranks were often linked together so as to make retreat impossible. Their priestesses cheered them on in battle, and, when prisoners were taken, cut their throats over a great bowl, and then, ripping them up, drew auguries from their entrails.

[Plan of the invaders.] The plan of the invaders was that one body, consisting of the Teutones, Ambrones, and Tugeni, should descend into Italy on the west, the Cimbri on the east. Whence the Teutones had come to join the Cimbri we do not know. They joined them in South Gaul. [The Ambrones.] The Ambrones may have been a clan of the Helvetii, as the Tugeni were. [Plan of Marius.] Marius waited for the western division at the confluence of the Isara and the Rhone, near the spot where Fabius had defeated the Arverni, his object being to command the two main roads into Italy, over the Little St. Bernard and along the coast. He did not follow the example of his old commander Scipio Aemilianus, in expelling soothsayers from his camp; for he had a Syrian woman, named Martha, with him to foretell the future. The soldiers had their own pet superstitions. They had caught two vultures, put rings on their necks and let them go, and so knew them again as they hovered over the army. When the barbarians reached the camp they tried to storm it. But they were beaten back, and then for six days they filed past with taunting questions, whether the Romans had any messages to send their wives. Marius cautiously followed, fortifying his camp nightly. They were making for the coast-road; and as they could not have taken their wagons along it, they were marching, as Marius had seen, to their own destruction. His strategy was masterly, for he was winning without fighting; but accident brought on an engagement. [Scene of the battle of Aquae Sextiae.] East of Aquae Sextiae (the modern Aix) Marius had occupied a range of hills, one of which is to this day called Sainte Victoire. The Arc flowed below. The soldiers wanted water, and Marius told his men that they might get it there if they wanted it, for he wished to accustom them to the barbarians' mode of fighting. Some of the barbarians were bathing; and on their giving the alarm, others came up, and a battle began. The first shock was between the Ambrones and Ligurians. The Romans supported the latter, and the Ambrones fled across the Arc to the wagons, where the women, assailing both pursuers and pursued with yells and blows, were slain with the men. So ended the first day's fight.

All night and next day the barbarians prepared for a final struggle. Marius planted an ambuscade of mounted camp-followers, headed by a few foot and horse in some ravines on the enemy's rear. [Circumstances of the battle.] He drew the legions up in front of the camp, and the cavalry went ahead to the plain. The barbarians charged up the hill, but were met by a shower of 'pila,' which the legionaries followed up by coming to close quarters with their swords. The enemy were rolled back down the hill, and at the same time with loud cries the ambuscade attacked them from behind. Then the battle became a butchery, in which, it was said, 200,000 men were slain, and among them Teutoboduus, their king. Others, however, say that he was taken prisoner, and became the chief ornament of Marius's triumph. Much of the spoil was gathered together to be burnt, and Marius, as the army stood round, was just lighting the heap, when men came riding at full speed and told him he was elected consul for the fifth time. The soldiers set up a joyful cheer, and his officers crowned him with a chaplet of bay. The name of the village of Pourrières (Campus de Putridis) and the hill of Sainte Victoire commemorate this great fight to our day, and till the French Revolution a procession used to be made by the neighbouring villagers every year to the hill, where a bonfire was lit, round which they paraded, crowned with flowers, and shouting 'Victoire, Victoire!'

[The Cimbri.] Meanwhile Catulus was waiting for the Cimbri on the east. A son of M. Aemilius Scaurus fled before them in the pass of Tridentum, and in 102 B.C., about the time of the battle of Aquae Sextiae, they poured down the valley on the east of the Athesis (Adige). [Catulus on the Adige.] Catulus was posted just below Verona on the west bank, with a bridge connecting

him with a smaller force on the other side. When the foe appeared his men took to flight; but the detachment on the east side stood its ground, and kept the enemy from crossing the bridge in pursuit. The Cimbri admired their bravery, and when they had forced the bridge let its defenders go. Pursuing Catulus, they cut him off from a river for which he was making, probably the Ticinus, though according to some, the Po. He then pretended to encamp on a hill as if for a long stay. The Cimbri dispersed over the country, and Catulus immediately came down, assaulted their camp and crossed the river, where he was joined by the victorious army of Gaul and by Marius, who had been to Rome. [Battle with the Cimbri, July 30, 101 B.C.] The village festival on the hill of Sainte Victoire was held in May. The battle with the Cimbri was fought on July 30, 101. More than a year therefore had elapsed since the Teutones were defeated. But it was the barbarians' custom not to fight in winter, and they were in a rich country which had not been invaded for a century, where they were revelling in unwonted comforts. So they spread themselves over the land as far as the Sesia; and when Marius came, they sent, it is said, and asked for land for the Teutones whom they were awaiting. [Story of the Cimbric embassy to Marius.] Marius replied that their brothers had all the land they wanted already. Upon which they requested him to name a field and a day for battle. Marius answered that Romans never consulted their foes on such points, but he would humour them, and named the Campi Raudii, near Vercellae. Such a story bears falsehood on the face of it. It is absurd to suppose that the Cimbri had not heard of the defeat of the Teutones, which had taken place more than a year before. Very likely they asked for land, and finding that they would only get hard blows, determined to bring matters to a crisis at once. Sulla's memoirs were Plutarch's authority for what followed, and Sulla hated Marius. [Story of Marius's jealousy of Catulus.] He said that Marius, expecting that the fighting would be on the wings, posted his own men there, that they might gain the glory, but that the brunt of the battle was borne by Catulus in the centre; and that such a dust rose that Marius was for a long time out of the battle, and knew not where he was. It seems that the barbarian cavalry feigned a flight, hoping to turn and take the Romans between themselves and their infantry. But the Romans drove back the cavalry on the infantry. [Circumstances of the battle.] However this may be, Marius had shown his usual good generalship. He had fed his men before the battle, and so manoeuvred that sun, wind, and dust were in the enemy's faces. His own men were in perfect training, and in the burning heat did not turn a hair. But the Northmen were fresh from high living, and could not bear up long. When they gave way, the same scenes as at Aquae Sextiae took place among the women. One hundred and twenty thousand men, it is said, were killed—among them the gallant Boiorix, their king— and 60,000 taken prisoners. Disputes rose as to who had really won the day. Marius generously insisted on Catulus sharing his triumph. But it was to him that the popular voice ascribed the victory, and there can be little doubt that the popular voice was right.
* * * * *

CHAPTER VI. THE ROMAN ARMY.

While Rome was trembling for the issue of the war with the Cimbri, she was forced to send an army elsewhere. [Slave revolts.] There was at this time another general stir among the slave population. There were risings at Nuceria, at Capua, in the silver mines of Attica, and at Thurii, and the last was headed by a Roman eques, named Minucius or Vettius. He wanted to buy a female slave; and, failing to raise the money which was her price, armed his own slaves, was joined by others, assumed the state and title of king, and fortified a camp, being at the head of 3,500 men. Lucullus, the praetor, marched against him with 4,400 men; but though superior in numbers, he preferred Jugurthine tactics, and bribed a Greek to betray Vettius, who anticipated a worse fate by suicide. [Second slave rebellion in Sicily.] But, as before, the fiercest outbreak was in Sicily. Marius had applied for men for his levies to Nicomedes, king of Bithynia, who replied that he had none to send, because the Roman publicani had carried off most of his subjects and sold them as slaves. Thereupon the Senate issued orders that no free member of an allied state should be kept as a slave in a Roman province. [Weakness of Licinius Nerva.] P. Licinius Nerva, governor of Sicily, in accordance with these orders, set free a number of Sicilian slaves; but, worked on by the indignation of the proprietors, he backed out of what he had begun to do, and, having raised the hopes of the slaves, caused an insurrection by disappointing them. He suppressed the first rebels by treachery. But he was a weak man, and delayed so long in attacking another body near Heraclea, that when he sent a lieutenant to attack them with 600 men they were strong enough to beat him. [Salvius elected king.] By this success they supplied themselves with arms, and then elected Salvius as their king, who found himself at the head of 20,000 infantry and 2,000 horse. With these troops he attacked Morgantia, and, on the governor coming to relieve it, turned on him and routed him; and by proclaiming that anyone who threw down his arms should be spared, he got a fresh supply for his men. [Athenion heads the slaves in the west.] Then the slaves of the west rose near Lilybaeum, headed by Athenion, a Cilician robber-captain before he was a slave, and a man of great courage and capacity, who pretended to be a magician and was elected king. [Salvius takes the name of Tryphon.] Salvius took the name of Tryphon, a usurper of the Syrian throne in 149. Athenion, deferring to his authority, became his general, and Triocala, supposed to be near the modern Calata Bellotta, was their head-quarters. In some respects this second slave revolt was a repetition of the first. As the Cilician Cleon submitted to the impostor Eunous, who called himself Antiochus, so now the Cilician Athenion submitted to the impostor Salvius, who called himself Tryphon. [Lucullus sent to Sicily, 103 B.C.] The outbreak had probably begun in 105, but it was not till 103 that Lucullus, who had put down Vettius, was sent to Sicily with 1,600 or 1,700 men. [Battle of Scirthaea.] Tryphon, distrusting Athenion, had put him in prison. But he released him now, and at Scirthaea a great battle was fought, in which 20,000 slaves were slain, and Athenion was left for dead. Lucullus, however, delayed to attack Triocala, and did nothing more, unless he destroyed his own military stores in order to injure his successor C. Servilius. To say that if he did so, such mean treason could only happen in a government where place depends on a popular vote, is a random criticism, for, though nominally open to all, the consulship was virtually closed, except to a few families, which retained now, as they had always done, the high offices in their own hands, and, when Marius forced this close circle, Metellus is said to have acted much as Lucullus did.

Servilius was incapable. Athenion, who at Tryphon's death became king, surprised his camp, and nearly captured Messana. [M'. Aquilius ends the war.] But, in 101, M'. Aquilius was sent out, and defeated Athenion and slew him with his own hand. A batch of 1,000 still remained under arms, but surrendered to Aquilius. He sent them to Rome to fight with wild beasts in the arena. They preferred to die by each other's swords there. Satyrus and one other were left last, and Satyrus after killing his comrade slew himself. The misery caused in Sicily by this long war, which ended in 100 B.C., may be estimated by the fact that, whereas Sicily usually supplied Rome with corn, it was now desolated by famine, and its towns had to be supplied with grain from Rome.

After this narration of the military events of the period to the beginning of the second century B.C., it is natural to consider the changes which Marius had effected in the army—the instrument of his late conquests. [Changes in the Roman army.] We cannot tell how many of the innovations now introduced were initiated by him, but they were introduced about this date. Before his time the Hastati, Principes, and Triarii, ranked according to length of service, had superseded the Servian classes. From his time this second classification also ceased. [Arms of the legionary.] Every legionary was armed alike with the heavy pilum—an iron-headed javelin 6 feet 9 inches long, the light pilum, a sword, and a coat of armour. Besides these he had to carry food and other burdens, which would vary according to the length and object of the march, such as stakes for encampment, tools, &c. [The 'Marian mules.'] Marius invented what were called 'Mariani muli' to ease the soldier—forked sticks, with a board at the end to bear the bundle, carried over the shoulders. Before his time the army had ceased to be recruited solely from Roman citizens. Not only had Italians been drafted into it, but foreign mercenaries were employed, such as Thracians, Africans, Ligurians, and Balearians. [The light troops auxiliaries.] After his time the Velites are not mentioned, and all the light-armed troop were auxiliaries. [The cohort the tactical unit.] Before his time the maniple had been the tactical unit. Now it was the cohort. [Composition of the legion.] A legion consisted of ten cohorts, each cohort containing three maniples, and each maniple two centuries. The legion's standard was the eagle, borne by the oldest centurion of the first cohort. Each cohort had its 'signum,' or ensign. [Standards.] Each maniple had its 'vexillum,' or standard. [Officers.] There were two centurions for each maniple, one commanding the first and the other the second century, and taking rank according to the cohort to which they belonged, which might be from the first to the tenth. The youngest centurion officered the second century of the third maniple of the tenth cohort. The oldest officered the first century of the first maniple of the first cohort, and was called 'primus-pilus,' and the 'primi ordines,' or first class of centurions, consisted of the six centurions of the first cohort. These corresponded to our non-commissioned officers, were taken from the lower classes of society, and were seldom made tribunes. [The tribunes.] The tribunes were six to each legion, were taken from the upper class, and after being attached to the general's suite, received the rank of tribune, if they were supposed to be qualified for it. The tribunes were originally appointed by the consuls. Afterwards they had been elected, partly by the people and partly by the consuls. Caesar superseded the tribunes by 'legati' of his own, to one of whom he would entrust a legion, and appointed some, but probably not all, of the tribunes, and Marius, it seems likely, did the same. [Numbers of the legion.] The normal number of a legion had been 4,200 men and 300 horse, but was often larger. [The pay.] The pay of a legionary was in the time of Polybius two obols a day for the private, four for a centurion, and six for a horse soldier, besides an allowance of corn. But deductions were made for clothing, arms, and food. Hence the law of Caius Gracchus (cf. p. 51); but from the first book of the Annals of Tacitus we find that such deductions long continued to be the soldier's grievance. Auxiliary troops received an allowance of corn, but no pay from Rome. [The engineers.] The engineers of the army were called Fabri, under a 'praefectus,' the 'Fabri Lignarii' having the woodwork, and the 'Fabri Ferrarii' the ironwork of the enginery under their special charge, [The staff.] and all were attached to the staff of the army, which consisted of the general and certain officers, such as the legati, or generals of division, and the quaestors, or managers of the commissariat. [The Cohors Praetoria.] One of the most significant changes that had sprung up of late years was one which was introduced by Scipio Aemilianus at Numantia—the institution of a body-guard, or Cohors Praetoria. It consisted of young men of rank, who went with the general to learn their profession, or as volunteers of troops specially enlisted for the post, who would often be veterans from his former armies. The term Evocati was applied to such veterans strictly, but also to any men specially enlisted for the purpose. [The equites.] It is probable that the equites no longer formed the cavalry of a legion, but only served in the general's body-guard, as tribunes and praefects, or on extraordinary commissions. The cavalry in Caesar's time appears to have consisted entirely of auxiliaries.

[Disinclination for service at Rome.] There had been for a long time among the wealthier classes a growing disinclination for service, and as the middle class was rapidly disappearing, there had been great difficulty in filling the ranks. The speeches of the Gracchi alluded to this, and it had been experienced in the wars with Viriathus, with Jugurtha, with Tryphon, and with the Cimbri. One device for avoiding it we have seen, by the orders issued to the captains of ships in Italian ports. Among Roman citizens, if not among the allies, some property qualification had been required in a soldier. [Marius enrols the Capite Censi.] Marius tapped a lower stratum, and allowed the Capite Censi to volunteer. To such men the prospect of plunder would be an object, and they would be far more at the bidding of individual generals than soldiers of the old stamp. Thus though obligation to service was not abolished, volunteering was allowed, and became the practice; and the army, with a new drill, and no longer consisting of Romans or even Italians, but of men of all nations, became as effective as of old, if not more so, and at the same time a body detached from the State. [The army ceases to be a citizen army.] The citizen was lost in the professional, and patriotism was superseded by the personal attachment of soldiers of fortune, who knew no will but that of their favourite commander or their own selfishness. Their general could reward them with money, and extort land for them from the State; and when Marius after Vercellae gave the franchise to two Italian cohorts, saying that he could not hear the laws in the din of arms, he was giving to what was becoming a standing army privileges which could not be conferred by a consul, but only by a king.

* * * * *

CHAPTER VII.SATURNINUS AND DRUSUS.

With such a weapon in his hand Marius came back to Rome, intoxicated with success. He thought his marches in two continents worthy to be compared with the progresses of Bacchus, and had a cup made on the model of that of the god. He spoke badly; he was easily disconcerted by the disapproval of an audience; he had no insight into the evils, or any project for the reformation, of the State. But the scorn of men like Metellus had made him throw himself on the support of the people from whom he sprang; and they, idolising him for his dazzling exploits as a soldier, looked to him as their natural leader, and the creator of a new era. Indeed it needed no stimulus from without to whet his ambitious cravings. That seventh consulship which superstition whispered would be surely his he had yet to win; and in all his after conduct he seems to have been guided by the most vulgar selfishness, which in the end became murderous insanity. But while he hoped to use all parties for his own advancement—a game in which he of all men was least qualified to succeed—other and abler politicians were bent on using him for the overthrow of the optimates.

[Saturninus.] The harangues of Memmius had shown that the spirit of the Gracchi was still alive in Rome; and now Lucius Apuleius Saturninus took up their revolutionary projects with a violence to which they had been averse, but for which the acts of their adversaries had become a fatal precedent. Of Saturninus himself we do not know much more than that he was an eloquent speaker, and a resolute though not over-scrupulous man at a time when to be scrupulous was equivalent to self-martyrdom or self-effacement. [Glaucia.] In something of the same relation in which Camille Desmoulins stood to Danton, Caius Servilius Glaucia, a wit and favourite of the people, stood towards the sombre and imperious Saturninus, and both hoped to effect their aims by the aid of Marius. If they are to be judged by their acts alone we can hardly condemn them.

[Defence of their policy.] They tried to do what the Gracchi had attempted before them, what Drusus attempted after them, and what, when they and Drusus had fallen, as the Gracchi had fallen, the Social War finally effected. No historian has given sufficient prominence to the fact that it was primarily a country movement of which each of these men was the leader; a movement of unbroken continuity, though each used his own means and had his own special temperament. If this is kept in view, we shall no longer consider with some modern historians that no event perhaps in Roman history is so sudden, so unconnected, and accordingly so obscure in its original causes as this revolt or conspiracy of Saturninus.

Like Caius Gracchus, Saturninus represented rural as opposed to urban interests, and the interests of the provinces as opposed to those of the capital. Like Caius, too, he endeavoured to conciliate the equites; but they had all the Roman prejudice against admitting Italians to a level with themselves, and the attempt to play off party against party utterly failed. In vain Saturninus tried to defy opposition by enlisting the support of the Marian veterans. The rich, the noble, and the city mob united against him; and when he seized the Capitol, it was to defend himself against all three. In the year 100 B.C. Marius was consul for the sixth time, Glaucia was praetor, and Saturninus was a second time tribune. A triumvirate so powerful might, if united, have overthrown the Constitution. But the vanity and vacillation of Marius were the best allies of the optimates; and it was no grown man, but Caius Julius Caesar, a child born in that same year, who was destined to subvert their rule. [The Lex Servilia. The equites and the judicia.] Saturninus had been instrumental in securing the election of Marius to his fifth consulship in 102, and it was about that time that the Lex Servilia was carried. This law defined the liability of Roman officials to trial for extortion in the provinces, and, by a process of elimination (for senators, workers for hire, and others were expressly declared ineligible), practically left to the equites the jurisdiction in such trials. Whether or no the law of Gracchus had been repealed by another Servilian law—that of Q. Servilius Caepio—we cannot say for certain. If so, the second Servilian law repealed the first. But, whether it restored power to the equites or only confirmed them in it, in theory it left the office of judex open to all citizens, for, while it excluded so many citizens that in practice the judicia were closed to all but the equestrian class, it did not assign the office to any one class in particular. It also provided that anyone not a citizen who won his suit against an official should by virtue of doing so obtain the citizenship. [Threefold purpose of the Lex Servilia.] So that we may trace in this law a threefold policy—an attempt (1) to relieve the provincials, by making prosecutions for extortion easy, and even putting a premium on them; (2) to conciliate the equites; (3) to pave the way for the overthrow of class jurisdiction by, nominally at least, leaving the judicia open to all who did not come under specified restrictions. Cicero inveighs against Glaucia as a demagogue of the Hyperbolus stamp. But there was more of the statesman than the demagogue in this law.

When Saturninus was a candidate for the tribunate, he and Glaucia are said to have set on men to murder Nonius, another candidate, who they feared might use his veto to thwart their projects. Marius had been previously elected consul, and supported Saturninus in his candidature, as Saturninus had supported him. [Personal reasons for Marius joining Saturninus.] Marius may have been induced to enter into this alliance by the desire to gratify a personal grudge, for the rival candidate had been the man he most detested, Q. Metellus; and the first measure of Saturninus was a compliment to him and a direct blow aimed at Metellus. [Agrarian law of Saturninus.] This was an agrarian law which would benefit the Marian veterans; and as it contained a proviso that any senator refusing to swear to observe it within five days should be expelled from the Senate, it would be sure to drive Metellus from Rome. But if there was diplomacy in this measure of Saturninus, there was sagacity also. What discontent was seething in Italy the Social War soon proved, and this was an attempt to appease it. Saturninus had previously proposed allotments in Africa; now he proposed to allot lands in Transalpine Gaul, Sicily, Achaia, and Macedonia, and to supply the colonists with an outfit from the treasure taken from Tolosa. Marius was to have the allotment of the land. [Difficulty about this agrarian law.] There is a difficulty as to these colonies which no history solves. They were Roman colonies to which only Roman citizens were eligible, and yet the Roman populace opposed the law. The Italians, on the contrary, carried it by violence. Some have cut the knot by supposing that, though the colonies were Roman, Italians were to be admitted to them. But there is another possible explanation. It is certain that many Italians passed as citizens at Rome. In 187 B.C. 12,000 Latins, passing as Roman citizens, had been obliged to quit Rome. In 95 B.C. there was another clearance of aliens, which was one of the immediate causes of the Social War. Fictitious citizens might have found it easy to obtain allotments from a consul whose ears, if first made deaf by the din of arms, had never since recovered their hearing. However this may be, it was the rural party which by violence procured a preponderance of votes at the ballot-boxes, and it was the town populace which resisted what it felt to be an invasion of its prerogative by the men from the country. [Exile of Metellus.] Marius is said to have got rid of Metellus by a trick. He pretended that he would not take the oath which the law demanded, but, when Metellus had said the same thing, told the Senate that he would swear to obey the law as far as it was a law, in order to induce the rural voters to leave Rome, and Metellus, scorning such a subterfuge, went into exile. [Corn-law of Saturninus.] Another law of Saturninus either renewed the corn-law of Caius Gracchus, or went farther and made the price of grain merely nominal. This law was no doubt meant to recover the favour of the city mob, which he had forfeited by his agrarian law. But Caepio, son, probably, of the hero of Tolosa, stopped the voting by force, and the law was not carried. [Law of treason.] The third law of Saturninus was a Lex de Majestate, a law by which anyone could be prosecuted for treason against the State, and which was not improbably aimed specially at Caepio, who was impeached under it. It seems at any rate certain that of these laws the agrarian was the chief, and the others subsidiary; in other words, that he and Glaucia were working together on an organized plan, and striving to admit the whole Roman world into a community of rights with Rome. They thought that with the Marian soldiers at their back they would be safer than Gracchus with his bands of reapers; and so they may have taken the initiative in violence from which, both by past events and the acts of men like Caepio, it was certain that the optimates would not shrink. It is difficult to apportion the blame in such cases. [Civil strife. Saturninus seizes the Capitol.] But when Glaucia stood for the consulship of 99, and his rival Memmius, a favourite with the people, was murdered, an attack was made on Saturninus, who hastily sent for aid to his rural supporters and seized the Capitol. He found then that in reckoning on Marius he had made a fatal blunder. That selfish intriguer had been alarmed by the popular favour shown to an impostor named Equitius, who gave out that he was the son of Tiberius Gracchus, and who, being imprisoned by Marius, was released by the people and elected tribune. He may have been jealous too of the popularity of Saturninus with his own veterans, and at the same time anxious to curry favour with the foes of Saturninus—the urban populace. [Marius turns on his friends.] So, instead of boldly joining his late ally, he became the general of the opposite party, drove Saturninus and his friends from the Forum, and, when they had surrendered, suffered them to be pelted to death in the Curia Hostilia where he had placed them. [Death of Saturninus and Glaucia.] Saturninus, it is said, had been proclaimed king before his death. If so he had at least struck for a crown consistently and boldly; and even if his attempt for the moment united the senatorial party and the equites, while the city mob stood wavering or hostile, he might nevertheless have forestalled the empire by a century had Marius only had half his enterprise or nerve. In an epoch of revolution it is idle to judge men by an ordinary standard. How far personal ambition and how far a nobler ideal animated Saturninus no man can say. Those who condemn him must condemn Cromwell too.

For the moment the power of the optimates seemed restored. The spectre of monarchy had made the men of riches coalesce with their old rivals the men of rank; and the mob, ungrateful for an unexecuted corn-law, chafed at Italian pretensions. Metellus, the aristocrat, was recalled to Rome amid the enthusiasm of the anti-Italian mob, and P. Furius was torn to pieces for having opposed his return. [Marius falls into disrepute.] Marius slunk away to the East, finding that his treachery had only isolated him and brought him into contempt; and there, it is said, he tried to incite Mithridates to war. Sextus Titius indeed brought forward an agrarian law in 99 B.C. But he was opposed by his colleagues and driven into exile. Two events soon happened which showed not only the embittered feelings existing between the urban and rural population, but also the sympathy with the provincials felt by the better Romans, and, as an inference, the miserable condition of the provincials themselves. [The Lex Licinia Minucia.] The first was the enactment, in 95 B.C., of the Lex Licinia Minucia, which ordered Latins and Italians resident at Rome to leave the city. [and the prosecution of Rutilius Rufus foreshadow the Social War.] The second was the prosecution and conviction of Publius Rutilius Rufus, nominally for extortion, but really because, by his just administration of the province of Asia, he had rebuked extortion and the equestrian courts which connived at it. Though most of the senators were as guilty as the equites, the mass, like M. Scaurus, who was himself impeached for extortion, would ill brook being forced to appear before their courts, and be eager to take hold of their maladministration of justice as a pretext for abrogating the Servilian law.

[Drusus attempts a reform.] One more attempt at reform was to be made, this time by one of the Senate's own members, but only to be once more defeated by rancorous party-spirit and besotted urban pride. Marcus Livius Drusus was son of the man whom the Senate had put forward to outbid Caius Gracchus. He was a haughty, upright man, of an impetuous temper—such a man as often becomes the tool of less courageous but more dexterous intriguers. M. Scaurus had been impeached for taking bribes in Asia, and it is said that in his disgust he egged on Drusus to restore the judicia to the Senate. Drusus was probably one of those men whom an aristocracy in its decadence not rarely produces. [Attitude of Drusus.] He disliked the preponderance of the moneyed class. He could not feel the vulgar Roman's antipathy to giving Italians the franchise, for he saw it exercised by men who were in his eyes infinitely more contemptible. He disliked also and despised the vices of his own order. Mistaking the crafty suggestions of Scaurus for a genuine appeal to high motives, flattered by it, and by the confidence of the Italians, he thought that he could educate his party, and by his personal influence induce it to do justice to Italy. But this conservative advocate of reform was not wily enough tactician for the times in which he lived, or the changes which he meditated. His attempts to improve on the devices of Saturninus and Gracchus were miserable failures; and the senators who used him, or were influenced by him, shrank from his side when they saw him follow to their logical issue the principles which they had advocated either for selfish objects or only theoretically.

[Main object of Drusus to aid the Italians.] Whether this is the true view of the character and position of Drusus or not, we may feel sure that he was in earnest in his advocacy of Italian interests, and that this was the main object of his reforms. [Sops to the mob: Depreciation of the coinage. Colonies. Corn-law.] To silence the mob at Rome, he slightly depreciated the coinage so as to relieve debtors, established some colonies—perhaps those promised by his father—and carried some law for distributing cheap grain. [Sop to the senate and equites.] Senators like Scaurus he courted by handing over the judicia once more to the Senate, while, by admitting 300 equites to the Senate, he hoped to compensate them for the wound which he thus inflicted on their material interests and their pride. The body thus composed was to try cases of judices accused of taking bribes. But the Senate scorned and yet feared the threatened invasion by which it would be severed into two antagonistic halves. The equites left behind were jealous of the equites promoted; and where Drusus hoped to conciliate both classes, he only drew down their united animosity upon himself. Even in Italy his plans were not unanimously approved. Occupiers of the public land, who had never yet been disturbed in their occupation—such as those who held the Campanian domain land—were alarmed by this plan of colonisation, which not only called in question once more their right of tenure, but even appropriated their land. But though the large land-owners were adverse to him, the great mass of the Italians was on his side; and it was by their help that he carried the first three of his laws, which he shrewdly included in one measure. Thus those who wanted land or grain were constrained to vote for the changes in the judicia also. But, as there was a law expressly forbidding this admixture of different measures in one bill, he left an opening for his opponents of which they soon took advantage. [Philippus opposes Drusus.] Chief of these opponents was the consul Philippus. When the Italians crowded into Rome to support Drusus, which they would do by overawing voters at the ballot-boxes, by recording fictitious votes, and by escorting Drusus about, so as to lend him the support which an apparent majority always confers, Philippus came forward as the champion of the opposite side. He seems to have been a turncoat, with a fluent tongue and few principles. He had no sympathy with the generous, if flighty, liberalism of the party of Drusus. No doubt it seemed to him weak sentimentalism; and he openly said that he must take counsel with other people, as he could not carry on the government with such a Senate. Accordingly he appealed to the worst Roman prejudices, viz. the selfishness of large occupiers and the anti-Italian sentiments of the mob. This explains his being numbered among the popular party, with which the Italian party was not now identical. Drusus, when his subsidiary measures had proved abortive, grew desperate. As his influence in the Senate waned he entered into closer alliance with the Italians, who, on their part, bound themselves by an oath to treat as their friend or enemy each friend or enemy of Drusus; and it is conjectured, from a fragment of Diodorus, that 10,000 of them, led by Pompaedius Silo, armed with daggers, set out for Rome to demand the franchise, but were persuaded to desist from their undertaking. [Drusus almost monarch.] Monarchy seemed once more imminent; and now, as in the case of Gracchus, it is impossible to say whether the attitude of the champion of reform was due to the force of circumstances or to settled design. But Philippus was equal to the occasion. He induced the Senate to annul the laws of Drusus already carried, and summoned the occupiers of the public land whom that law affected, to come and confront the Italians in Rome. [Assassination of Drusus.] A battle in the streets would have no doubt ensued; but it was prevented by the assassination of Drusus, who was one evening stabbed mortally in his own house. It is said that when dying he ejaculated that it would be long before the State had another citizen like him. He seems to have had much of the disinterested spirit of Caius Gracchus, though with far inferior ability; and, like him, he left a mother Cornelia, to do honour by her fortitude to the memory of her son. That year the presentiment of coming political convulsions found expression in reports of supernatural prodigies, while 'signs both on the earth and in the heavens portended war and bloodshed, the tramp of hostile armies, and the devastation of the peninsula.'

* * * * *

CHAPTER VIII.THE SOCIAL WAR

In a previous chapter the relations now existing between Rome and her dependents have been described. For two centuries the Italians had remained faithful to Rome through repeated temptations, and even through the fiery trial of Hannibal's victorious occupation. But the loyalty, which no external or sudden shock could snap, had been slowly eaten away by corrosives, which the arrogance or negligence of the government supplied. It is clear from the episode of Drusus that there was as wide a breach between Italian capitalists and cultivators, as there had been between Roman occupiers and the first clamourers for agrarian laws. So, at the outbreak of the war, Umbria and Etruria, whence Philippus had summoned his supporters, because the farmer class had been annihilated and large land-owners held the soil, remained faithful to Rome. But where the farmer class still flourished, as among the Marsi, Marrucini, and the adjacent districts, discontent had been gathering volume for many years. No doubt the demoralisation of the metropolis contributed to this result; and, as intercourse with Rome became more and more common, familiarity with the vices of their masters would breed indignation in the minds of the hardier dependents. Who, they would ask themselves, were these Scauri, these Philippi, men fit only to murder patriots and sell their country and themselves for gold, that they should lord it over Italians? Why should a Roman soldier have the right of appeal to a civil tribunal, and an Italian soldier be at the mercy of martial law? Why should two Italians for every one Roman be forced to fight Rome's battles? Why should insolent young Romans and the fine ladies of the metropolis insult Italian magistrates and murder Italians of humbler rank? This was the reward of their long fidelity. If here and there a statesman was willing to yield them the franchise, the flower of the aristocracy, the Scaevolae and the Crassi, expelled them by an Alien Act from Rome. They had tried all parties, and by all been disappointed, for Roman factions were united on one point, and one only—in obstinate refusal to give Italians justice. The two glorious brothers had been slain because they pitied their wrongs. So had Scipio. So had the fearless Saturninus. And now their last friend, this second Scipio, Drusus, had been struck down by the same cowardly hands. Surely it was time to act for themselves and avenge their benefactors. They were more numerous, they were hardier than their tyrants; and if not so well organized, still by their union with Drusus they were in some sort welded together, and now or never was the time to strike. For the friends of Drusus were marked men. Let them remain passive, and either individual Italians would perish by the dagger which had slain Drusus, or individual communities by the sentence of the Senate which had exterminated Fregellae.

[Outbreak of the Social War.] The revolt broke out at Asculum. Various towns were exchanging hostages to secure mutual fidelity. Caius Servilius, the Roman praetor, hearing that this was going on at Asculum, went there and sharply censured the people in the theatre. He and his escort were torn to pieces, the gates were shut, every Roman in the town was slain, and the Marsi, Peligni, Marrucini, Frentani, Vestini, Picentini, Hirpini, the people of Pompeii and Venusia, the Iapyges, the Lucani, and the Samnites, and all the people from the Liris to the Adriatic, flew to arms; [The allies who remained faithful to Rome.] and though here and there a town like Pinna of the Vestini, or a partisan like Minutius Magius of Aeclanum, remained loyal to Rome, all the centre and south of Italy was soon in insurrection. Perhaps at Pinna the large land-owners or capitalists were supreme, as in Umbria and Etruria, which sided with Rome, as also did most of the Latin towns, the Greek towns Neapolis and Rhegium, and most of Campania, where Capua became an important Roman post during the war. [The rebels demand the franchise.] The insurgents, emboldened by the swift spread of the rebellion, sent to demand the franchise as the price of submission. But the old dogged spirit which extremity of danger had ever aroused at Rome was not dead. [Rage of the equites. The law of Varius.] The offer was sternly rejected, and the equites turned furiously on the optimates, or the Italianising section of the optimates, to whose folly they felt that the war was due. With war the hope of their gains was gone; and, enraged at this, they took advantage of the outbreak to repay the Senate for its complicity in the attempt of Drusus to deprive them of the judicia. Under a law of Varius, who is said by Cicero to have been the assassin of Drusus and Metellus, Italian sympathisers were brought to trial, and either convicted and banished, or overawed into silence. Among the accused was Scaurus. But now, as ever, that shifty man emerged triumphant from his intrigues. He aped the defence of Scipio, and retired not only safe, but with a dignity so well studied that but for his antecedents it might have seemed sincere. A Spaniard accused him, he said, and Scaurus, chief of the Senate, denied the accusation. Whether of the twain should the Romans believe?

[Perils of the crisis.] For such prosecutions there was indeed some excuse, for the prospect was threatening. Mithridates might at any moment stop the supplies from Asia. The soldiers of the enemy were men who had fought in Roman armies and been trained to Roman discipline; they were led by able captains, and were more numerous than the forces opposed to them. And yet the war must be a war of detachments, where numbers were all-important. It was no time for hesitation about purging out all traitors or waverers. But the courts that tried other cases were closed for the time. The distributions of grain were curtailed. The walls were put in order. Arms were prepared as fast as possible. A fleet was collected from the free cities of Greece and Asia Minor. Levies were raised from the citizens, from Africa, and from Gaul. Lastly, in view of the inevitably scattered form which the fighting would take, each consul was to have five lieutenants. [Generals of Rome.] Lupus was to command in the northern district, from Picenum to Campania. Among the generals who acted under him were the father of Pompeius Magnus, and Marius. Samnium, Campania, and the southern district fell to Lucius Julius Caesar, and among the five officers who went with him were also two men of mark, Publius Licinius Crassus and Sulla. We shall see how by an exhaustive process the Romans, after a series of defeats, were at last driven to employ as generals-in-chief the two rivals who were now subordinates and were thus carefully kept aloof.

[Corfinium the capital of the confederates.] The confederates on their part were equally energetic. They had chosen as their capital Corfinium, on the river Aternus (Pescara), because of its central position with reference to the insurrection, and soon made it evident that the Roman franchise was no longer the limit to their aspirations, but that they aimed at the conquest of Rome herself. [Measures of the confederates.] They called their capital Italica. In it they built a forum, and fortified its walls. They issued a new coinage. They chose two consuls, twelve praetors, and a senate of five hundred, and gave the franchise to every community in arms on their side. They mustered an army of 100,000 men, and entrusted the command against Lupus in the north and west to Pompaedius Silo, with six lieutenants under him; the command against Caesar in the south and east was given to a noted Samnite, named Caius Papius Mutilus.

It is easier to get a general idea of the war than of its details, though the latter are not without interest. The results of the first year were, in spite of some victories, most unfavourable to Rome. The insurgents were encouraged. The insurrection had spread to Umbria and Etruria, and the Romans had at one time almost despaired. [General survey of the war.] But in council they retrieved what they had lost in the camp. A most politic concession of the franchise checked all further disaffection in the very nick of time. The revolt in Umbria and Etruria was speedily suppressed, and at the close of the second year of the war, B.C. 89, the insurrection itself was virtually at an end. For, though the Sulpician revolution at Rome prevented its absolute extinction, and some embers of it still lingered for five years more, and though Roman forces were still required after 89 B.C. among the Sabines in Samnium, in Lucania, and at Nola, the war as a war ended in that year. [Twofold division of the war.] Consequently we may divide it into two periods, each well defined and each consisting of a year, the first in which the confederate cause triumphed and Marius lost credit; the second in which the cause of Rome triumphed, and Sulla enhanced his reputation and became the foremost man at Rome.

[B.C. 90. First year of the war. Attempt on Asculum by Pompeius.] The war began, as was natural, with an attempt to take Asculum. But the townsmen, manning the walls with the old men past service, surprised Cnaeus Pompeius by a sally, and defeated him. [Pompeius defeated and driven into Firmum.] Subsequently he was again defeated at Faleria and driven into Firmum, a Latin colony which held out for Rome. There he stayed till Servius Sulpicius came to his help. [Pompeius, relieved by Sulpicius, besieges Asculum.] On the approach of Sulpicius he sallied out. The enemy, taken in front and rear, was routed, and Pompeius began the siege of Asculum. It was not taken till the next year, 89, and only after a desperate battle before its walls. Judacilius, who had come to relieve the town of which he was a native, though the day was lost, forced his way inside the walls, and held out for several months longer. Finally, when it was impossible to protract the defence, he had a pile of wood made, and a table placed on it at which he feasted with friends. Then, taking poison, he had the pile fired. When the Romans got in they took fearful vengeance, slaying all the officers and men of position, expelling the rest of the inhabitants, and confiscating their property. Such was the fate of the ringleaders of the rebellion. [The confederates assail the towns which cling to Rome.] As Asculum was the first object of Roman vengeance, so the confederates directed their first efforts against the towns in their neighbourhood which refused to join them. Silo assailed Alba and Mutilus Aesernia. The consul Caesar, sending ahead Marcellus and Crassus into Samnium and Lucania, followed in person as soon as he could. Put he was beaten by Vettius Scato in Samnium with the loss of 2,000 men. [They take Aesernia and are joined by Venafrum.] Venafrum thereupon revolted; and, though one account says that Sulla relieved Aesernia, it was at best only a partial or a temporary relief, for it capitulated before the close of the year. How the siege of Alba ended we do not know. Defeat after defeat was now announced at Rome. [Perperna defeated.] Perperna lost 4,000 men, and most of his other soldiers threw away their arms on the battlefield. For this Lupus deprived him of his command and attached his troops to those of Marius. [Crassus defeated. Grumentum taken by the confederates.] Crassus was beaten in Lucania and shut up in Grumentum, which was besieged and taken. [Story of the generosity of some slaves.] A pleasant story is told about some slaves of this town. They had deserted to the confederates, and when the town was taken made straight for the house where they had lived and dragged their mistress away, telling people they were going to have their revenge on her at last. And so they saved her. [Nola taken by the confederates.] While the troops of Crassus were cooped up in Grumentum Mutilus descended into Campania and obtained possession of Nola by treason. Two thousand soldiers also went over to him. The officers remained loyal and were starved to death. [Town after town won by the confederates.] Stabiae, Salernum, Pompeii, Herculaneum, and probably Nuceria were taken in quick succession; and, with his army swollen by deserters and recruits from the neighbourhood, Mutilus laid siege to Acerrae. Caesar hastened to relieve it. But Canusium and Venusia had joined the insurgents, and in Venusia Oxyntas, son of Jugurtha, had been kept prisoner by the Romans. Mutilus now put royal robes on him, and the Numidians in Caesar's army, when they saw him, deserted in troops, so that Caesar was forced to send the whole corps home. [Caesar gains the first success for Rome; but is afterwards defeated.] But out of this misfortune came the first gleam of success which had as yet shone on the Roman arms. Mutilus ventured to attack Caesar's camp, was driven back; and in the retreat the Roman cavalry cut down 6,000 of his men. Though Marius Egnatius soon afterwards defeated Caesar, this victory in some sort dissipated the gloom of the capital; and while the two armies settled again into their old position at Acerrae, the garb of mourning was laid aside at Rome for the first time since the war began. Lupus and Marius meanwhile had marched against the Marsi. Marius, in accordance with his old tactics against the Cimbri, advised Lupus not to hazard a battle. But Lupus thought that Marius wanted to get the consulship next year and reserve for himself the honours of the war. So he hastened to fight, and, throwing two bridges over the Tolenus, crossed by one himself, leaving Marius to cross by the other. [Lupus defeated by the Marsi.] As soon as the consul had reached the opposite bank, an ambuscade set by Vettius Scato attacked him, and slew him and 8,000 of his men. Their bodies, floating down the river, told Marius what had happened. Like the good soldier that he was, he promptly crossed and seized the enemy's camp. This disaster happened June 11, B.C. 90, and caused great consternation in Rome. But at Rome small merit was now discerned in any success gained by the veteran general, and Caepio, who had opposed Drusus and was therefore a favourite with the equites, was made joint commander in the north. It was a foolish choice. The prudence of Marius and a victory over the Peligni gained by Sulpicius were neutralised by the new general's rashness. Pompaedius Silo, who must have been a thoroughly gallant man, came in person to the Roman camp, bringing two young slaves whom he passed off as his own children and offered as hostages for the sincerity of the offer he made, which was to place his camp in Caepio's hands. [Caepio defeated and slain by Silo.] Caepio went with him, and Pompaedius, running up a hill to look out, as he said, for the enemy, gave a signal to men whom he had placed in ambush. Caepio and many of his men were slain, and at last Marius was sole commander. He advanced steadily but warily into the Marsian country. Silo tauntingly told him to come down and fight, if he was a great general. [Prudence of Marius.] 'Nay,' replied Marius, 'if you are a great general, do you make me.' At length he did fight; and, as he always did, won the day. In another battle the Marrucinian leader, and 6,000 of the Marsi were slain. [Success of Sulla.] But Sulla was at that time co-operating with Marius, having apparently, when the Romans evacuated most of Campania, marched north to form a junction with him; and beside his star that of Marius always paled. Marius had shrunk from following the enemy into a vineyard. Sulla, on the other side of it, cut them off. Not that Marius was always over-cautious. Once in this war he said to his men, 'I don't know which are the greatest cowards, you or the enemy, for they dare not face your backs, nor you theirs.' But everything he now did was distrusted at home; and while some men disparaged his successes, and said that he was grown old and clumsy, others were more afraid of him than of the enemy, with whom indeed there was some reason to think that he had too good an understanding. [A secret understanding, possibly, between Marius and the confederates.] For once, when his army and Silo's were near each other, both generals and men conversed, cursing the war, and with mutual embraces adjuring each other to desist from it. If the story be true, it is a sufficient reason for the Senate's conduct, inexplicable except by political reasons, in not employing Marius at all in the following year.

[Revolt of the Umbrians and Etruscans.] It was probably at the close of this year that the revolt of the Umbrians and Etruscans took place, and that Plotius defeated the Umbrians, and Porcius Cato the Etruscans. On a general review of this piecemeal campaign it is plain that the Romans had been worsted. On the main scene of war, Campania, they had been decisively defeated, and the country was in the enemy's power. In Picenum and the Marsian territory the balance was more even; but Lupus and Caepio had been slain, Perperna and Pompeius had been defeated, and on the whole the confederates had carried off the honours of the war. [Results of the first year of the war.] Now Umbria was in insurrection, Mithridates was astir in Asia, and there were symptoms of revolt in Transalpine Gaul. A selfish intriguer like Marius might very likely have thought of throwing in his lot with the Italians, for theirs seemed to be the winning side. But on honester men such considerations produced quite another effect. [The party of Drusus revives.] The party of Drusus took heart again, and appealed to the results of the war as a proof of his patriotic foresight and of the moderation of his counsels. They got the administration of the Varian Law into their own hands, and turned it against its authors, Varius himself being exiled. The consul Caesar had personal reasons for being disquieted with the war, if the story of Orosius be true, that, when he asked for a triumph for his victory at Acerrae, the Senate sent him a mourning robe as a sign of what they thought of his request. [The Lex Julia.] In any case he was the author of that Lex Julia which really terminated the Social War. [Various accounts of the law.] There are different accounts given of this law. According to Gellius it enfranchised all Latium, by which he must mean to include all the Latin colonies. According to Cicero it enfranchised all Italy except Cisalpine Gaul. According to Appian it enfranchised all the Italians still faithful. In any case those enfranchised were not to be enrolled in the old tribes lest they should swamp them by their votes, but in eight new ones, which were to vote only after the others. [The Lex Plautia Papiria.] The Lex Julia was immediately followed by the Lex Plautia Papiria, framed by the tribunes M. Plautius Silvanus and C. Papirius Carbo. This law seems to have been meant to supplement the other. The Lex Julia rewarded the Italians who had remained faithful. The Lex Plautia Papiria held out the olive branch to the Italians who had rebelled. It enfranchised any citizen of an allied town who at the date of the law was dwelling in Italy, and made a declaration to the praetor within sixty days. In the same year, and in connexion no doubt with these measures, the Jus Latii was conferred on a number of towns north of the Po, by which every magistrate in his town might, if he chose, claim the franchise. Some of the free allies of Rome did not look upon the Lex Julia as a boon. Heracleia and Neapolis hesitated to accept it, the latter having special privileges, such as exemption from service by land, which it valued above the franchise. Probably these towns and Rhegium made a special bargain, and, while accepting the franchise, retained their own language and institutions. [Effects of these laws.] The general result of the legislation was this. All Italy and all Latin colonies in Cisalpine Gaul, together with all allied communities in Cisalpine Gaul south of the Po, received the franchise. All the other Cisalpine towns north of the Po received the Jus Latii. A general amnesty was in fact offered; and though the provisions as to the new tribes were unsatisfactory, its effect was soon apparent.

[B.C. 89 The second year of the war.] [Successes of Pompeius in the north.] The consuls for 89 were Lucius Porcius Cato, who took command of the army in the Marian district, and Cnaeus Pompeius, who retained the command in Picenum. Caesar was succeeded in Campania by Sulla. Flushed with hope, the confederates opened the campaign by despatching 15,000 men across the Apennines to join the Etruscan insurgents. But Pompeius intercepted and slew 5,000 of them, and dispersed the rest, who, even if they had reached Etruria, would have found that they had come on a bootless errand. He followed up this success by blow after blow. One of his lieutenants, Sulpicius, crushed the Marrucini at Teate. Another, Q. Metellus Piso, subdued the Marsi. Pompeius in person fought a great battle before Asculum, as before related, and captured the town; and in the following year the Peligni and Vestini submitted to him.

[Successes of Cosconius in the south-east.] In the south-east of Italy, Cosconius, the praetor, burnt Salapia in Apulia, received the submission of Cannae, and besieged Canusium. Marius Egnatius came to its aid; but though he at first drove back Cosconius to Cannae, he or his successor was defeated and slain in another fight, and Cosconius became master of all Apulia and the Iapygian peninsula, which he laid waste with fire and sword.

[Successes of Sulla in the south-west.] While the Roman supremacy was thus re-established all along the east coast, Sulla, in Campania, was equally triumphant. He recovered Stabiae in April, and his lieutenant, T. Didius, took Herculaneum in June. Didius, however, lost his life in the assault. Sulla next besieged Pompeii, defeated Cluentius who came to its aid, again defeated him between Pompeii and Nola, and a third time at the gates of Nola, where Cluentius was slain. About this time Aulus Postumius Albinus, while in charge of the fleet, was murdered by his own men, recruits probably whom he was bringing from Rome to Sulla's army. Sulla pardoned the mutineers, saying that he knew they would wipe out their crime by their bravery, and they did so in the fights with Cluentius. By such politic clemency and never-varying good fortune Sulla bound the army to his own interests.

Leaving Nola behind him, he crossed the Hirpinian frontier and marched on Aeclanum. The townsmen, who were expecting a Lucanian reinforcement that day, asked for time to deliberate. Sulla gave them an hour, and occupied the hour in heaping vine osiers round the wooden walls. Not choosing to be burnt the townsmen surrendered, and Sulla sacked the place. He then marched northwards into Samnium. The mountain-passes were held by Mutilus, who hemmed in Sulla near Aesernia. Sulla pretended to treat for peace, and, when the enemy were off their guard, marched away in the night, leaving a trumpeter to sound all the watches as if the army was still in position. He seems to have defeated Mutilus after this, and, leaving Aesernia behind as he had left Nola, finally, before going home to sue for the consulship of 88 B.C., stormed Bovianum. He had managed the campaign in a bold and able way, where less daring generalship might have failed.

[First Bovianum, and then Aesernia, becomes the confederate capital.] As the insurrection was thus being stamped out on either coast, Bovianum had become the capital of the insurgents instead of Corfinium. Now Bovianum was taken, and Aesernia became its centre. The occupation of the Hirpinian territory cut off the Samnites from the South of Italy, where the Lucanians and Bruttians remained in arms. Except for some trifling operations, which Pompeius had to carry out in order to complete the pacification of his district, all that was now left for the commanders of 88 was to crush the rebels in these two isolated divisions, and the war would be at an end. [B.C. 88. Desperation of the confederates.] The rebels indeed prepared for a desperate resistance. Five generals were appointed, Pompaedius Silo, the Marsian, at their head; and, by enrolling slaves and calling out fresh levies, the Samnites mustered an army of 50,000 men. Once more, almost single-handed, they prepared to strive with their old enemy for the sovereignty of Italy. The gallant Silo signalised his appointment by recovering Bovianum, but he was soon afterwards slain. He is said to have been defeated in a great battle by Mamercus Aemilius, and to have fallen in it. Appian says that Metellus defeated him in Iapygia; Orosius, that Sulpicius defeated him in Apulia. However that may be, with him the last gleam of hope for the Samnite cause faded away. They made, it is said, a treaty with Mithridates; but long before that king could have reached Italy, if he had been able to make the attempt, there would have been no allies to support him. In Lucania Aulus Gabinius, made rash by some successes, assaulted the confederate camp, but was repulsed and slain. Lamponius, the Lucanian general, remained master of the country, and attempted to take Rhegium, with the view of crossing over

to Sicily and renewing the rebellion there. But the attempt failed. [Revolution at Rome, and the part taken by the insurgents in it.] Nola, however, still held out in Campania; and now there occurred a revolution at Rome which postponed the final subjugation of the insurgents till after the battle of the Colline Gate. For convenience and clearness the part taken by them in this revolution may be here summarised. Sulla, as consul, was besieging Nola when he was recalled to Rome by the Sulpician revolution and his election to the command against Mithridates. A Samnite army had come to relieve it, but had been defeated by Sulla. Three Roman corps still remained to keep the Samnites in check and besiege Nola, under Claudius, Metellus, and Plotius. It was to Nola that Cinna came, and seduced a large portion of the besiegers to follow him to Rome. Upon this the insurgents suddenly found themselves, instead of hunted desperadoes, courted as allies by two parties. The Senate again offered the terms of the Lex Plautia Papiria to all in arms, and some accepted them. But the Nolans, when Metellus was recalled and the long siege was then raised in 87 B.C., marched out and burnt Abella. The Samnites demanded, as the price of their assistance, that the prisoners, spoils, and deserters should be restored, and that they and the Romans who had joined them should receive the franchise. The Senate refused, and the Samnites at once joined Cinna and Marius, who were pledged not only to give the franchise, but also to enrol all the new voters in the old tribes; a measure which was ratified by the Senate in the year of Cinna's last consulship, 84 B.C. On Sulla's return to Italy they with the Lucanians, who had meanwhile been practically independent, were the most eager supporters of Marius's son. [Pontius of Telesia.] In 82 Pontius of Telesia, at the head of a Samnite force, with the desperate hardihood inspired by centuries of hatred, marched straight on Rome, and the city was saved only by Sulla's victory at the Colline Gate. Three days after the battle Sulla massacred all his prisoners. He knew that death alone could disarm such implacable foes. The Samnite name, he said, with its cold ferocity, must be erased from the earth, or Rome could never rest. The Samnites evacuated Nola in the year 80 B.C., and then their last great leader, C. Papius Mutilus, having fled in disguise to his wife at Teanum, was disowned by her and slew himself. [Fate of Samnium.] Sulla carried his threats into effect. He captured Aesernia, and spread a desolation all around, from which the country has never recovered to this day. Then, and not till then, the stubborn resistance of the most relentless foes of Rome was finally suppressed.
* * * * *

CHAPTER IX.SULPICIUS.

The terrible disintegration which the Social War had brought on Italy was faithfully reproduced in Rome. There, too, every man's hand was against his neighbour. Creditor and debtor, tribune and consul, Senate and anti-Senate, fiercely confronted each other. Personal interests had become so much more prominent, and old party-divisions were so confused by the schemes of Italianising politicians, aristocratic in their connexions, but cleaving to part at least of the traditional democratic programme, that it is very hard to see where the views of one faction blended with those of another and where they clashed. [The Sulpician revolution difficult to understand.] Still harder is it to dissect the character of individuals; to decide, for instance, how far a man like Sulpicius was swayed by disinterested principles, and how far he fought for his own hand. We need not make too much of the fact that he appealed to force, because violence was the order of the day, and submission to the law simply meant submission to the law of force. But there are some parts of his career apparently so inconsistent as almost to defy explanation which in any case can be little more than guesswork.
[Sulpicius.] Publius Sulpicius Rufus was now in the prime of life, having been born in 124 B.C.

He was an aristocrat, an orator of great force and fire, and a friend of Drusus, whose views he shared and inherited. Cicero speaks of him in no grudging terms. 'Of all the speakers I have heard Sulpicius was the grandest, and, so to speak, most tragic. Besides being powerful, his voice was sweet and resonant. His gestures and movements, elegant though they were, had nothing theatrical about them, and his oratory, though quick and fluent, was neither redundant nor verbose.' [Financial crisis at Rome.] The year before his tribunate had been a turbulent one at Rome. The Social War and Asiatic disturbances had brought about a financial crisis. Debtors, hard pressed by their creditors, invoked obsolete penalties against usury in their defence, and the creditors, because the praetor Asellio attempted to submit the question to trial, murdered him in the open Forum. The debtors responded by a cry for tabulae novae, or a sweeping remission of all debts. Of these debtors many doubtless would belong to the lower orders; but, from a proposal of Sulpicius made the next year, it appears probable that some were found in the ranks of the Senate. War had made money 'tight,' to use the phraseology of our modern Stock Exchange, and reckless extravagance could no longer be supported by borrowing.

[Sulpicius the successor of Drusus.] Sulpicius inherited the policy of Drusus, which was to reconstruct the Senatorial Government on an Italian basis. Like Drusus he had to conciliate prejudices in order to carry out his design. Plutarch says that he went about with 600 men of the equestrian order, whom he called his anti-Senate. No doubt it was to please these equites, who would belong to the party of creditors, that he proposed that no one should be a senator who owed more than 2,000 denarii. No doubt, too, he would have filled the vacancies thus created by the expulsion of reckless anti-Italian optimates, from the ranks of these equites, just as Drusus had done. [He attempts to remodel the government.] Just like Drusus, too, he had to court the proletariate, and this he did by proposing to enrol freedmen in the tribes. This, as they were generally dependent on men of his own order, he could do without prejudice to the new-modelled aristocracy which he was attempting to organize. He also proposed to grant an amnesty to those who had been exiled by the Lex Varia, hoping, no doubt, to gain more by the adherents who would return to Rome than he would lose by the return of men like Varius himself. He had opposed such an amnesty before; but on such a point he might have easily changed his views, especially if a strong cry was being raised by the friends of the exiles. He had a personal feud with the Julian family, because he had opposed Caesar's illegal candidature for the consulship; but, having fortified himself by such alliances, he proceeded to carry out the main design of Drusus, namely, the complete enfranchisement of the Italians. [Pro-Italian measure of Sulpicius.] This, perhaps, would be especially distasteful to the Julii, as superseding the Lex Julia and the Lex Plautia Papiria, which to them, no doubt, seemed ample and more than ample concessions. Sulpicius, on the other hand, and the minority of the Senate which sided with him, saw that under the cover of clemency a grievous wrong was being done. For not only were the Italians who had submitted since the terms of the Lex Plautia took effect without the franchise, but from the fact of their rebellion they had lost their old privileges as allied States. Even those who had benefited by these concessions had benefited only in name. As they voted in new tribes, their votes were valueless, and often would not be recorded at all; for a majority on most questions would be assured long before it came to their turn to vote. To a statesman imbued with the views of Drusus such a distribution of the franchise must have seemed impolitic trickery; and, like Drusus, Sulpicius resorted to questionable means in order to gain the end on which he had set his heart. Rome was thus broken up into two camps, not as of yore broadly marked off by palpable distinctions of rank, property, or privilege, but each containing adherents of all sorts and conditions, though in the Senate the opponents of Sulpicius had the majority. When Sulpicius proposed to enrol the Italians in the old tribes, the consuls proclaimed a justitium, or suspension of all public business for some religious observances. It is said by some modern writers that the object of Sulpicius in proposing to enrol the Italians in the old tribes was to secure the election of Marius to the command against Mithridates. It is certain, indeed, that Marius longed for it. [Attitude of Marius.] Daily he was to be seen in the Campus Martius exercising with the young men, and, though old and fat, showing himself nimble in arms and active on horseback—conduct which excited some men's good-humoured sympathy, but shocked others, who thought he had much better go to Baiae for the baths there, and that such an exhibition was contemptible in one of his years. Sulpicius may have thought Marius quite fit for the command, and was warranted in thinking so by the events of the Social War; but there is no more ground for supposing that the election of Marius was his primary object than for considering Plutarch's diatribe a fair estimate of his character. [Connection of Marius and Sulpicius explained.] He was the friend and successor of Drusus, and his alliance with Marius was a means to the end which in common with Drusus he had in view, and not the end itself. This consideration is essential to a true understanding of the politics of the time, and just makes the difference whether Sulpicius was a petty-minded adventurer or deliberately following in the lines laid down for him by a succession of statesmen. [Street-fighting.] To the manoeuvre of the consul he replied by a violent protest that it was illegal. Rome was being paraded by his partisans—3,000 armed men, and there was a tumult in which the lives of the consuls were in danger. One, Pompeius Rufus, escaped, but his son was killed. The other, Sulla, annulled the justitium, but is said to have got off with his life only because Marius generously gave him shelter in his own house. In these occurrences it is impossible not to see that the consuls were the first to act unfairly. Sulpicius had been intending to bring forward his laws in the regular fashion. They thwarted him by a trick. Whether he in anger gave the signal for violence, or whether, as is quite as likely, his Italian partisans did not wait for his bidding, the blame of the tumult lay at the door of the other side. In such cases he is not guiltiest who strikes the first blow, but he who has made blows inevitable.

[The Sulpician laws carried by force.] The laws of Sulpicius were carried. [Sulla flies to the army, which marches on Rome.] Sulla fled to the army; and, perhaps, it was only now that Sulpicius, knowing or thinking that he knew that Sulla would march on Rome, carried a resolution in the popular assembly for making Marius commander in the east. Two tribunes were accordingly sent to the camp at Nola to take the army from Sulla. His soldiers immediately slew them; and, burning for the booty of Asia and attached to their fortunate leader, they, when without venturing to hint at the means by which he could avenge it, he complained of the wrong done to him, clamorously called on him to lead them to Rome. All his officers, except one quaestor, left him; but he set out with six legions and was joined by Pompeius on the way. Two praetors met him and forbade his advance. They escaped with their lives, but the soldiers broke their fasces and tore off their senatorial robes. A second and a third time the Senate sent to ask his intentions. 'To release Rome from her tyrants,' was the grim reply. Then he vouchsafed an offer that the Senate, Marius, and Sulpicius should meet him in the Campus Martius to come to terms. If this meant that he would come with his army at his back, it was an absurd proposal. If it meant that he would come alone, it was a falsehood. In either case it was a device to fritter away time. [Sulla's astuteness and superstition.] For all the while that he was bandying meaningless messages he continued his onward march. He had sacrificed, and the soothsayer Postumius, when he saw the entrails, had stretched out his hands to him, and offered to be kept in chains for punishment after the battle if it was not a victory. He, too, had himself seen a vision of good omen. Bellona, or another goddess, had, he dreamed, put a thunderbolt in his hands, and, naming his enemies one by one, bidden him strike them, and they were consumed to ashes.

Again envoys came from the Senate forbidding him to come within five miles of Rome. Perhaps they still felt as secure in the immemorial freedom of the city from military rule as the English Parliament did before Cromwell's coup d'état. Again he amused them, and no doubt himself also, with a falsehood, and, professing compliance, followed close upon their heels. With one legion he occupied the Caelian Gate, with another under Pompeius the Colline Gate, with a third the Pons Sublicius, while a fourth was posted outside as a reserve. Thus, for the first time, a consul commanded an army in the city, and soldiers were masters of Rome. [Street-fighting.] Marius and Sulpicius met them on the Esquiline and, pouring down tiles from the housetops, at first beat them back. But Sulla, waving a burning torch, bade his men shoot fiery arrows at the houses, and drove the Marians from the Esquiline Forum. Then he sent for the legion in reserve, and ordered a detachment to go round by the Subura and take the enemy in the rear. In vain Marius made another stand at the temple of Tellus. In vain he offered liberty to any slaves that would join him. He was beaten and fled from the city. Thus Sulla, having by injustice provoked disorder, quelled it by the sword, and began the civil war. Sulpicius, Marius, and ten others were proscribed, and Sulla is said to have still further stimulated the pursuit of Marius by setting a price on his head. [Sulpicius slain.] Sulpicius was killed at Laurentum, and, according to Velleius Paterculus, Sulla fixed up the eloquent orator's head at the Rostra, a thing not unlikely to have been done by a man to whose nature such grim irony was thoroughly congenial. [Stories of Sulla.] He evinced it on this occasion in another way, which may have suggested to Victor Hugo his episode of Lantenac and the gunner. He gave the slave who betrayed Sulpicius his freedom, and then had him hurled from the Tarpeian Rock. After this he set to work to restore such order as would enable him to hasten to the east.

[Why Sulla left Italy.] Various explanations have been offered to account for his moderation at this conjuncture, and for his leaving Italy precisely when his enemies were again gathering for an attack. But the true one has never yet, perhaps, been suggested. Who was it that had made him supreme at Rome? The army. What had been the bribe which had won it over? A campaign in Asia under the fortunate Sulla. Without that army he was powerless, nay, he was a dead man. Therefore it was absolutely necessary to execute his pledge to the army, which would have no keen desire to encounter its countrymen in Italy. No doubt he coveted the glory and spoil of the Asiatic command; but it is absurd to suppose that he would have quitted Italy now of his own free will. He had no choice in the matter. He was bound hand and foot by his promises to the soldiers; and all that he could do was by plausible moderation to win as many friends, conciliate as many foes, as possible, throw on Cinna, whom he could not hope to keep quiet, the guilt of perjury, and trust to fortune for the rest. This is a probable and consistent view of what now took place at Rome; and every other account makes out Sulla to have been either inconsistent, which he never was, for he was always uniformly selfish; or patriotic, which he never was, if patriotism consists in sacrificing private to public considerations; or indifferent, which he was in principle but never in practice, unless where his own interests were not threatened and only the suffering of others involved.

[Sulla's measures.] His first measure was to annul the Sulpician laws. Secondly, to relieve the debtors, some colonies were established, and a law was passed about interest, the terms of which we do not know. Thirdly, the Senate, thinned by the Social War and the Varian law, was recruited by 300 optimates. Fourthly, because Sulpicius had resisted the proclamation of a justitium—that device by which the Senate had virtually, though not legally, retained in its own hands the power of discussing any measure before it was submitted to the people—therefore for the future no measure was to be submitted to the people till it had been previously discussed by the Senate. In other words, the Senate was now confirmed by law in a privilege which it had hitherto only exercised by the employment of a fiction. Fifthly, the votes were to be taken, not in the Comitia Tributa, but in the Comitia of Centuries. Sixthly, the five classes were no longer to have an equal voice, but the first class was, as in the Servian constitution, to have nearly half the votes. As the first class consisted of those who had an estate of 100,000 sesterces, this ordinance changed the democracy into a timocracy, transferring the power from the people generally to the wealthier classes: but, considering how voting had been manipulated of late, it was perhaps a measure due to the Senate quite as much as to Sulla. On the whole he legislated as little as he could and proscribed as few as he could. [Opposition to Sulla.] But he tried to get two of his partisans, Servius and Nonius, elected consuls for the year 87. Instead of them, however, L. Cornelius Cinna, a determined leader of the populares, was elected; and though Cnaeus Octavius, his colleague, was one of the optimates, he was not Sulla's creature. In another quarter his arrangements were thwarted even more unpleasantly. He had got a decree framed by the people, giving the army of the north to his friend Q. Pompeius Rufus, and recalling Cn. Pompeius Strabo. But the latter procured the assassination of the former, and remained at the head of the army. Still Sulla showed no resentment. A tribune named Virginius was threatening to prosecute him. But he contented himself with making Cinna ascend the Capitol with a stone in his hand, and, throwing it down before a number of spectators, solemnly swear to observe the new constitution. Then, leaving Metellus in Samnium and Appius Claudius at Nola, he hurried to Capua, and embarking at Brundusium felt, no doubt, that if he must pay his debt to the army before the army would commit fresh treasons for him, it was not unpleasant now to be forced away from the wasps' nest which he had stirred up round him at home. And so, making a virtue of a necessity, he sailed with a light heart from the chance of assassination at Rome to fame and fortune in the East.

* * * * *

CHAPTER X. MARIUS AND CINNA.

Meanwhile what had become of Marius? Already a halo of legend was gathering round his name, and all Italy was ringing with his adventures. When he had fled from Rome (not sorry now, we may be sure, that he had gone through his late exhibitions in the Campus Martius), he had sent his son to some of his father-in-law's farms to get necessary provisions. Young Marius was overtaken by daylight, before he could get to his father-in-law's farm, and pack the things up, and was nearly caught by those on his track. But the farm-bailiff saw them in time, and, hiding him in a cart full of beans, yoked the teams, and drove him to Rome. [Ostia.] There young Marius went to his wife's house, and, getting what he wanted, set out at nightfall for Ostia, and finding a ship starting for Africa, went aboard. His father had not waited for his return. He too had embarked at Ostia for Africa with his son-in-law. But now in his old age the sea was not so kind to him as when, in his bold and confident youth, he had sailed to sue for his first consulship from the very land to which he was now flying. A storm came on, and the ship was blown southwards along the coast. Marius begged the captain to keep clear of Tarracina, because Geminius, a leading man there, was his bitter foe. [Circeii.] But the storm increased; Marius was sea-sick, and they were forced to go ashore at Circeii (Monte Circello). Some herdsmen told them that horsemen had just been there in pursuit; so they spent the night in a thick wood, hungry, and tortured by anxiety. Next day they went to the coast again, and Marius implored the men to stand by him, telling them that when he was a child an eagle's nest fell into his lap, with seven young ones in it, and the soothsayers had said that it meant that he should attain to the highest honours seven times. [Minturnae.] About two miles and a half from Minturnae they spied some horsemen making towards them; and, plunging into the sea, they swam towards some merchantmen near the shore. Two slaves swam with Marius, keeping him up, and he got into one ship, and his son-in-law into the other, while the horsemen shouted to the crew to put ashore, or throw Marius overboard. The captains consulted together, and a terrible moment it must have been for the fugitives. But the spell of the Cimbric victories was potent still, and the captains replied that they would not give up Marius. So the soldiers rode off in a rage. But the sailors, having so far acted generously, were anxious to get rid of their dangerous guest, and, landing at the mouth of the Liris, on pretence of waiting for a fair wind, told Marius to go ashore and get some rest, and, while he was lying down, sailed away. Half stupified, he scrambled through bogs, and dykes, and mud, till he came to an old man's cottage, and begged the owner to shelter a man who, if he escaped, would reward him beyond his hopes. The man told him that he could hide him in a safer place than his cottage; and, showing him a hole by the riverside, covered him up in it with some rushes. But he was soon rudely disturbed. Geminius was on his trail, and Marius heard some of his emissaries loudly threatening the old man for hiding an outlaw. In his terror Marius stripped and plunged into the river, and so betrayed himself to the pursuers, who hauled him out naked and covered with mud, and gave him up to the magistrates of Minturnae. By these he was placed under a strong guard in the house of a woman named Fannia. She, like Geminius, had a personal grudge against him, for in his sixth consulship he had fined her four drachmas for ill-conduct. But now when she saw his misery she forgot her resentment, and did her best to cheer him. Nor was this difficult, for the stout heart of Marius had never failed him. He told Fannia that, as he was coming to her house, an ass had come out to drink at a neighbouring fountain, and, fixing its eyes steadily on him, had brayed aloud and frisked vivaciously, whence he augured that he would find safety by sea. The magistrates, however, had resolved to kill him, and sent a Cimbrian to do the deed, for no citizen would do it. The man went armed with a sword into the gloomy room where Marius lay. But soon he ran out crying, 'I cannot slay Marius.' He had seen eyes glaring in the darkness, and had heard a terrible voice say, 'Darest thou slay Caius Marius?' His heart had failed him; he had thrown down the sword and fled. Either the magistrates now changed their minds, or the people forced them to let Marius go, or perhaps Fannia connived at his escape. Plutarch says that the people escorted him to the coast, and, when they came to a sacred grove, called the Marician Grove, which no man might enter, but which it would take a long time to go round, an old man had led the way into it, saying that no place was so sacred but that it might be entered to save Marius. [Aenaria.] In some way he reached the coast where a friend had secured a vessel, and being driven by the wind to Aenaria (Ischia), he there found his son-in-law and sailed for Africa.

[Eryx.] Want of water forced them to put in at Eryx on the N.W. of Sicily; but the Roman quaestor there was on the look-out, and killing sixteen of the crew nearly took Marius. Landing at Meninx (Jerbah), the fugitive heard that his son was in Africa too, and had gone to Hiempsal, King of Numidia, to ask for aid, upon which he set sail again and landed at Carthage. [Carthage.] The Roman governor there sent to warn him off from Africa. Marius was dumb with indignation, but on being asked what answer he had to send, replied, so ran the story, 'Go and say you have seen Caius Marius sitting on the ruins of Carthage.'

Hiempsal meanwhile had been keeping young Marius in a sort of honourable captivity. But, according to a story similar to that told of Thomas à Becket's father, a damsel of the country had fallen in love with his handsome face, and helped him to escape. [Circina.] Father and son now

retired to Circina (Kerkennah), where news soon reached him which brought him back to Italy. [Counter-revolutions at Rome.] Hardly had Sulla left Brundusium when the truce which he had patched up was broken. Cinna being bribed, as was said probably without foundation, with 300 talents, had demanded that the Italians lately enfranchised should be enrolled in the old tribes. [Cinna.] We do not know very much about Cinna, but we do seem to gather that he was bold, resolute, not ungenerous or bloodthirsty; and it cannot be too strongly insisted on that, like Saturninus, and Sulpicius, and Drusus, he was only demanding justice. [Street-fighting. Cinna driven from Rome.] Octavius opposed him, and, hearing that Cinna's partisans were threatening the tribunes in the Forum, he charged down the Via Sacra with a band of followers, and dispersed them, and a great number of Cinna's followers were slain. On this Cinna left Rome, and, joined by Sertorius, whom we shall hear of again, went round the towns mustering his friends. The Senate declared his consulship to be void, and elected L. Cornelius Merula in his place. [His cause espoused by the Campanian army.] Cinna, with characteristic audacity, instantly hastened to the army in Campania; and, rending his clothes and throwing himself on the ground, so worked on the pity of the soldiers that they lifted him up, and told him he was consul still, and might lead them where he pleased. [Marius lands in Etruria.] Then, visiting the Italian towns, he obtained many recruits; and, hearing that Marius had landed in Etruria (perhaps on his invitation), he agreed to act in concert with him, in spite of the opposition of Sertorius.
[The Senate summons Pompeius from Picenum.] Meanwhile Octavius and Merula had fortified the city, had sent for troops from Cisalpine Gaul, and had summoned the proconsul Pompeius from Picenum. Pompeius came and halted at the Colline Gate. It was suspected that he was waiting to join the successful side. With him was his son, afterwards called 'the Great,' who now showed of what stuff he was made by putting down a mutiny against his father and baffling a plot for his own assassination. [Marius sacks Ostia, and he, Sertorius, and Cinna hem Rome in.] Marius, with a band of Moors, and the slaves whom he had collected from the Etrurian field-gangs, was admitted by treachery into Ostia and sacked the town. Cinna marched to the right bank of the Tiber, opposite the Janiculum. Sertorius held the river above the city, and a corps was sent to Ariminum to prevent any help coming from North Italy. [The Senate summons Metellus, and courts the alliance of the Samnites.] At this crisis the Senate sent for Metellus and tried to obtain the aid of the Samnites, who, as we have seen, joined Marius and Cinna. The treachery of a tribune in command of the Janiculum gave the Marians admission to the city. But they were driven out again, and might even have been dislodged from the Janiculum had not Pompeius persuaded Octavius to check the pursuit. Pompeius was playing a waiting game, ready to join the strongest, or crush both parties, as he saw his chance. And now within the city starvation set in, and a pestilence spread. Marius had blocked up the Tiber, and occupied the outlying towns on which the communications of the capital depended. Nor could the Senate trust its own troops. [Death of Pompeius.] Pompeius was killed by a thunder-bolt—not less suspicious than that which slew Romulus—and his body had been torn from the bier, and dragged through the streets by the people. [Disaffection in the Senate's troops.] The soldiers of Octavius cheered Cinna when he marshalled his troops opposite them near the Alban Mount. Moreover the leaders themselves were at variance. Octavius, seeing the humour of his men, was afraid to fight, but would concede nothing. Metellus wished for a compromise. Both armies were now outside the city, the pestilence probably having driven the Marians to withdraw. But Marius had command of the Via Appia, the Tiber, and most of the neighbourhood; and the famine became sorer in Rome. [Incompetence of Octavius and Metellus.] The soldiers wished Metellus to take the command from Octavius, and, on his refusal, deserted in crowds to the enemy. So also did the

slaves, to whom Octavius would not promise freedom, as Cinna gladly did. [The Senate submits to Cinna.] At last the Senate sent to make terms with Cinna; but while they were stickling about acknowledging his title of consul, he advanced to the gates. Then they surrendered at discretion, only begging him to swear to shed no blood. Cinna, refusing to be bound by this condition, promised that he would not voluntarily do so. For he saw by his side the grim figure of the man to whom he had given pro-consular powers, who had already taunted him with weakness for conferring with the Senate at all, and in whose sullen, unshorn face he read a craving for vengeance which nothing but blood would satisfy.

[A massacre at Rome.] When Cinna entered the city, Marius, with savage irony, said that an outlaw had no business within the walls, and he would not come in till the sentence had been formally rescinded by a meeting of the people in the Forum. But the gates, when once he had passed them, were closed, and for five days and five nights Rome became a shambles. Appian says that Marius and Cinna had both sworn to spare the life of Octavius. But Marius was never a liar, and the story is false on the face of it; for just before this Appian relates how, when Cinna had promised to be merciful, Marius would make no sign. [Death of Octavius.] Octavius is said to have seated himself in his official chair, dressed in his official robes, on the Janiculum, and to have awaited the assassins there. His head was fastened up in front of the Rostra in emulation of the ghastly precedent set by Sulla. He was an obstinate, dull man; and if this burlesque of the conduct of the senators when the Gauls took Rome was really enacted, the theatrical display must have been cold comfort for those of his party on whom his incapacity brought ruin. [Chief victims of the massacre.] [The Caesars.] Among the latter were the brothers Caesar, Caius, who had sought to be consul before he was praetor, and had been denounced for it by Sulpicius, and Lucius, the conqueror at Acerrae and author of the Julian law. [Publius Crassus.] Publius Crassus, consul in 97, and one of Caesar's lieutenants in the Social War, fled with his son, and when overtaken first stabbed his son and then himself. [Marcus Antonius.] Marcus Antonius, the great forensic orator, was so odious to Marius that the latter, on hearing that he was taken, wished, so the story runs, to go and kill him with his own hand. Antonius was in hiding, and was betrayed by the indiscretion of a slave, who, being questioned by a wine-seller why he was buying more or better wine than usual, whispered to him that it was for Marcus Antonius. On the soldiers coming to kill him, he pleaded so eloquently for his life that they wept and would not touch him. But their officer, who was waiting below, impatiently came up and cut off his head with his own hand. Lucius Merula opened his veins, and so bled to death. His crime was that he had been made consul when Cinna was deposed. His last act seems odd to us, but pathetically bespoke the man's piety and recalls the last scene in the life of Demosthenes. He wrote on a tablet that he had taken off his official cap when opening his veins, so as to avoid the sacrilege of a flamen of Jupiter dying with it on his head. [Catulus.] Marius had behaved generously once to Q. Lutatius Catulus, his old colleague against the Cimbri; but Catulus had helped to drive him into exile, and there was to be no second mistake of that sort. 'He must die,' he said, when the relatives of Catulus pleaded for his life. It is not unlikely that disease, and drinking, and his late hardships had made the old man insane. He had been occasionally good-natured in former days; now he seemed to gloat in carnage. For every sneer cast at him, for every wrong done to him in past years, he took a horrible revenge. When Cinna had summoned him, he had said that he would settle the question of enrolment in the tribes once for all. He wished not to select victims, but to massacre all the leading optimates. Sertorius begged Cinna to check the slaughter. Cinna did try to curb the outrages of the slave bands; but he dared not break with Marius, whom he named as joint consul with himself for the year 86. But as soon as his colleague was dead, he and

Sertorius surrounded the ruffians and killed them to a man.

[Death of Marius.] Marius did not live much longer. He had had his revenge. He had gained his seventh consulship. It is said that, telling his friends that after such vicissitudes it would be wrong to tempt fate further, he took to his bed and after seven days died. He drank hard, was seized with pleurisy, and in his last hours became delirious. He fancied that he was in Asia, and by shouts and gestures cheered on the army of his dreams, and with 'such a stern and iron-clashing close' died January 13 or 17. He was more than seventy years old, and had enjoyed his seventh consulship for either thirteen or seventeen days.

Lucius Valerius Flaccus succeeded Marius as consul, and passed a law making one-fourth of a debt legal tender for payment of it; and probably in the same year the denarius was restored to its standard value. A census was also held, which would include the new Italian citizens, and Philippus, whose opposition to Drusus on this very question had helped to kindle the Social War, was censor. [Settlement of Italian disabilities by Cinna.] Cinna, as he was pledged to do so, must have carried some measure for enrolling the Italians in the old tribes; but we can only conjecture what was actually done. Sulpicius had already carried such a measure, but it had been probably revoked by Sulla before he left Italy. In 84, just before his return, the Senate, it is said, gave the Italians the right of voting, and distributed the libertini, or freed slaves, among the thirty-five tribes. Perhaps this was a formal ratification of what had been passed before under Cinna's coercion.

Cinna was now all-powerful at Rome. For four successive years, 87 to 84 B.C., he was consul; and with the exception of Asia, Macedonia, Greece, and Africa, where Metellus had escaped and was in arms, the whole Roman world was at his feet. But he did not know how to use his power. He may have removed the restrictions on grain, and did proclaim Sulla and Metellus outlaws; but, though he should have bent every energy to hinder Sulla's return, he did worse than nothing, and, instead of Sertorius, sent the incapable Flaccus and the ruffian Fimbria against the general who had just taken Athens and defeated Archelaus. The miscarriage of their enterprise will be told in the next chapter. When Cinna suddenly became alive to the fact that the avenger was at hand, and that either he must act promptly or Sulla would be in Rome, he hastened to Ancona, where he sent one division of the army across to the opposite coast. But the second division was driven back by a storm; and the soldiers then dispersed, saying that they would not fight against their own countrymen. On this the rest of the army refused to embark. Cinna went to harangue them, and one of his lictors in clearing a way struck a soldier. Another soldier struck him. [Cinna slain at Ancona.] Cinna told his lictors to seize this second mutineer, and in the tumult that arose Cinna was slain. Plutarch says that the troops murdered him because he was suspected of having killed Pompeius, and that, when he tried to bribe a centurion with a signet-ring to spare him, the centurion replied that he was not going to seal a bond but slay a tyrant. But Cinna probably died as he lived, a brave man, and one who could not have held ascendency for so long, and over men like Sertorius, had he not been an able as well as a brave man.

* * * * *

CHAPTER XI. THE FIRST MITHRIDATIC WAR.

Events have been anticipated in order to relate the close of Cinna's career. But it is time now to say what Sulla had been doing, and who that Mithridates was whose name for so long had been formidable at Rome.

After the defeat of the northern hordes and the suppression of the second slave revolt, there was a war with the Celtiberi in Spain, in 97, in which Sertorius showed himself already an adroit and bold officer. [Sertorius in command against the Celtiberi.] He was in winter quarters at Castulo (Cazlona), and his men were so disorderly that the Spaniards were emboldened to attack them in the town; Sertorius escaped, rallied those soldiers who had also escaped, marched back, and after putting those in the town to the sword, dressed his troops in the dead men's clothes, and so obtained admission to another town which had helped the enemy. But the hero of the campaign was Titus Didius, afterwards Caesar's lieutenant in the Social War. He had some hard fighting and captured Termesus, the chief town of the Arevaci, and Colenda.—He earned his triumph by other means also. There was a town near Colenda, the inhabitants of which the Romans wished to destroy. Didius told them that he would give them the lands of Colenda, and they came to receive their allotments. As soon as they were within his lines, his soldiers set on them and slew them all.

[Africa.] In 96 B.C. Ptolemaus Apion bequeathed Cyrene—a narrow strip of terraced land on the north coast of Africa, situated between the Libyan deserts and the Mediterranean—to Rome. The Romans did not refuse the legacy; but they took no trouble to govern the country. The cities of Cyrene were declared to be free. In other words, while nominally subject to Rome, so that she might interfere when she pleased, they were left to govern themselves. Such government was no government; but it was in accordance with the deliberate policy of the senatorial party.

[Crimes and intrigues of Mithridates.] It was in the same year that Mithridates committed the first of the series of crimes which eventually brought him into collision with Rome. His sister had married the King of Cappadocia. Mithridates assassinated him. Nicomedes, King of Bithynia, seized Cappadocia and married the widowed sister of Mithridates. Having slain one brother-in-law, Mithridates expelled the other, and set on the throne his sister's son. But when his nephew refused to welcome home Gordius, the man who had murdered his father, Mithridates marched against and assassinated him. Then he set on the throne his own son, to whom he gave his nephew's name, and made Gordius his guardian. Him the Cappadocians expelled, and raised to the throne another nephew of Mithridates; but Mithridates instantly drove him from power. Nicomedes now appealed to the Senate, and produced, as he asserted, a third nephew of Mithridates as a claimant for the crown. To support his assertion he sent his wife to Rome to swear she had had three sons. Mithridates, as if in burlesque of the imposture, sent Gordius to swear that the youth on the throne was son of a Cappadocian king who had died more than thirty years before. The Senate decided as a lion might between two jackals quarrelling over a carcase. It took Cappadocia from Mithridates and Paphlagonia from Nicomedes, and declared both countries free. But the Cappadocians clamoured for a king, and so, in 93, the Senate appointed Ariobarzanes I. Mithridates then stirred up Tigranes, King of Armenia, to expel Ariobarzanes, who fled to Rome. Sulla was sent to restore him, and did so in 92, after defeating the Cappadocians under Gordius and the Armenians. [The Romans come in contact with the Parthians.] It was when he was on this mission that the Romans and Parthians confronted each other for the first time. The Parthians sent an embassy to ask for the alliance of Rome. Three chairs were set for Ariobarzanes, Sulla, and Orobazus; and Sulla, who was only propraetor, took the central seat. This incensed the Parthian king; and he revenged himself not on Sulla, but on the unfortunate Orobazus, whom he put to death. A Chaldean in the Parthian's suite, after studying Sulla's face, predicted great things for him; which pleased Sulla as much as it would have done Marius, for he believed in his luck just as his rival did in his seventh consulship. But when he came home he was impeached for taking bribes from Ariobarzanes, and no doubt he had made his trip which was so gratifying to his pride not less profitable also, and had had his appetite whetted for a second taste of eastern treasures. Mithridates, meanwhile, was brooding over his humiliation and meditating revenge. He went on a journey incognito through the Roman province of Asia and Bithynia, intending to attack both if he found himself strong enough. When he came back he found that his wife, who was also his sister, had been unfaithful to him, and he put her to death. He had now murdered a wife, a sister, a brother, and a nephew. He had also imprisoned his mother, and was equally merciless to his sons, his daughters, and his concubines. At his death, it is said, a paper was found in which he had foredoomed his most trusted servants, and he slew all the inmates of his harem in order to hinder them from falling into his enemies' hands.

[Early years of Mithridates.] His whole history is in fact one long record of sensuality, treachery, and murder. From his earliest years he had breathed, as it were, an atmosphere of assassination. His father had been assassinated when he was eleven years old. His guardians and even his own mother had then plotted to assassinate him. They placed him on a wild horse, and made him perform exercises with the javelin on it. When his precocious vigour defeated their hopes, they tried to poison him. But by studying antidotes he made his body poison-proof, or at least was reputed to have done so, and, flying from his enemies, lived for seven years through all the hardships of a wild and wandering life, in which he never slept under a roof, and hunted and fought with wild beasts, to emerge in manhood a very tiger himself for strength, and beauty of body, and ferocity of disposition, a tyrant who spared neither man in his ambition nor woman in his lust. [His physical vigour.] His stature was gigantic, his strength and activity such as took captive the imagination of the East. He could, it was believed, outrun the deer; out-eat and out-drink everyone at the banquet; strike down flying game unerringly; tame the wildest steed, and ride 120 miles in a day. Twenty-two nations obeyed him, and he could speak the dialect of each. A veneer of Greek refinement was spread thinly over the savage animalism of the man. [Pseudo-civilisation of his court.] He was a virtuoso, and had a wonderful collection of rings. He maintained Greek poets and historians, and offered prizes for singing. He had shrewdness enough to employ Greek generals, but not enough to keep him from being grossly superstitious. [His kingdom and how it was acquired.] For twenty years (110-90 B.C.) he had been with never-resting activity extending his empire, before the Romans assailed him. He had inherited from his ancestors the kingdom of Pontus, or Cappadocia on the Pontus, which had been one of the two satrapies into which Cappadocia was divided at the time of the Macedonian conquest. Mithridates IV. had married a princess of the Greek race, the sister of Seleucus, King of Syria. His grandfather had conquered Sinope and Paphlagonia, as far as the Bithynian frontier. His father had helped the Romans in the third Punic War, had been styled the friend of Rome, and had been rewarded with the province of Phrygia nominally for his services against Aristonicus, the pretender to the kingdom of Attalus, but had been deprived of it afterwards when it was found out that really it had been put up for auction by Manius Aquillius, who was completing the subjugation of the adherents of the pretender. The boundaries of Pontus at his accession cannot be strictly defined. On the east it stretched towards the Caucasus and the sources of the Euphrates, Lesser Armenia being dependent on it. On the south and south-west its frontiers were Cappadocia and Galatia. On the west nominally Paphlagonia was the frontier, for the grandfather of Mithridates had been induced by the Romans to promise to evacuate his conquests. But Sinope was then, and continued to be, the capital of the Pontic kingdom, and both Paphlagonia and Galatia were virtually dependent. This was the territory to which Mithridates was heir, and which, true to the policy of his father and grandfather, he constantly strove by force or fraud to extend. [Mithridates extends his kingdom.] To the east of the Black Sea he conquered Colchis on the Phasis, and converted it into a satrapy. To the north he was hailed as the deliverer of the

Greek towns on that coast and in the region now known as the Crimea, which from the constant exaction of tribute by barbarous tribes were, in the absence of any protectorate like that of Athens, falling into decay. By sea, and perhaps across the Caucasus by land, Mithridates sent his troops under the Greek generals Neoptolemus and Diophantus. Neoptolemus won a victory over the Tauric Scythians at Panticapaeum (Kertch), and the kingdom of Bosporus in the Crimea was ceded to his master by its grateful king. Diophantus marched westwards as far as the Tyras (Dneister), and in a great battle almost annihilated an army of the Roxolani, a nomadic people who roamed between the Borysthenes (Dneiper) and the Tanais (Don). By these conquests Mithridates acquired a tribute of 200 talents (48,000_l_.), and 270,000 bushels of grain, and a rich recruiting ground for his armies. [His alliance with Tigranes.] On the east he annexed Lesser Armenia, and entered into the closest alliance with Tigranes, King of Greater Armenia, which had lately become a powerful kingdom, giving him his daughter Cleopatra in marriage. If the allies had any defined scheme of conquest, it was that Mithridates should occupy Asia Minor and the coast of the Black Sea, and Tigranes the interior and Syria. How the King intrigued and meddled in Cappadocia and Bithynia has been previously related; and when he had marched into Cappadocia it was at the head of 80,000 foot, 10,000 horse, and 600 scythed chariots.

Such was the history, the power, and the character of the great potentate who had yielded to the demands of Sulla, the propraetor, but who now awaited the attack of Sulla, the proconsul, with proud disdain. Much, indeed, had happened since the year 92 to justify such feelings. Hardly had Sulla reinstated Ariobarzanes when Tigranes drove him out again, and restored the son of Mithridates; while in Bithynia the younger son of Nicomedes, Socrates, appeared in arms against his elder brother, Nicomedes II., who on his father's death had been acknowledged as king by Rome. Socrates had soldiers from Pontus with him; but Mithridates, though his hand was plain in these disturbances, outwardly stood aloof; and the Senate, sending Manius Aquillius to restore the two kings, ordered Mithridates to aid him with troops if they were wanted. [Mithridates submits to Aquillius.] The king submitted as before, not, indeed, sending troops, but without resisting, and as a proof of his complacency put Socrates to death. This happened in the year 90, when Rome was pressed hardest by the Italians, and at first sight it seems astonishing that he should not have seized on so favourable a moment. But in those days news would travel from the west of Italy to Sinope but slowly and uncertainly, and Mithridates would have the fate of Antiochus in mind to warn him how the foes of the great republic fared, and the history of Pergamus to testify to the prosperity of those who remained its friends. Sulla's proud tone in 92 would not have lessened this impression; and, before he appealed to force, the crafty king hoped to make his position securer by fraud. Partly, therefore, from real awe, partly because he was not yet ready, he obeyed Aquillius as he had obeyed Sulla. But Aquillius, who had once put up Phrygia to auction, knew what pickings there were for a senator when war was afoot in Asia, and perhaps may have had the honester notion that, as Mithridates was sure to go to war soon, it was for the public as well as for his private interest to act boldly and strike the first blow. So he forced the reluctant Bithynian king to declare war, and to ravage with an army the country round Amastris while his fleet shut up the Bosporus. Still Mithridates did not stir; all that he did was to lodge a complaint with the Romans, and solicit their mediation or their permission to defend himself. [Aquillius forces on a war.] Aquillius replied that he must in no case make war on Nicomedes. It is easy to conceive how such an answer affected a man of the king's temper. He instantly sent his son with an army into Cappadocia. But once more he tried diplomacy. [Ultimatum of Mithridates.] Pelopidas, his envoy, came to Aquillius, and said that his master was willing to aid the Romans against the Italians if the Romans would forbid Nicomedes to attack him, their ally. If not, he wished the alliance to be formally dissolved. Or there was yet another alternative. Let the commissioners and himself appeal to the Senate to decide between them. The commissioners treated the message as an insult. Mithridates, they said, must not attack Nicomedes, and they intended to restore Ariobarzanes. Possibly the conduct of Aquillius was due to his having been heavily bribed by Nicomedes, who must have felt that when the Romans were gone he would be like a mouse awaiting the cat's spring; for it is difficult to imagine the foolhardiness which without some such tangible stimulus would at that moment have plunged him into war.

[War begun. Energy of Mithridates.] But when once the die was cast, Mithridates threw himself into the war with the energy of long-suppressed rage. He sent to court the alliance of Egypt and the Cretan league, to whom he represented himself as the champion of Greece against her tyrant. He tried to stir up revolts in Thrace and Macedonia. He arranged with Tigranes that an Armenian army should co-operate with him, leaving him the land it occupied, but carrying off the plunder. He gave the word, and a swarm of pirate ships swept the Mediterranean under his colours. He summoned an army of 250,000 foot, 40,000 horse, and 130 scythed chariots, a fleet of 300 decked vessels, and 100 other ships called 'Dicrota' with a double bank of oars. He formed and armed in Roman fashion a foreign contingent, in which many Romans and Italians enlisted; and he placed able Greek generals, Archelaus and Neoptolemus, over his troops. [Forces of Rome.] To meet this formidable array the Romans had a fleet off Byzantium, the army of Nicomedes, which was still between Sinope and Amastris, and three corps, each of 40,000 men, but composed for the most part of hastily organized Asiatics; one under Cassius between Bithynia and Galatia, another under Aquillius between Bithynia and Pontus, and a third under Oppius in Cappadocia. The war was decided almost in a single battle. [Victory of Mithridates over Nicomedes.] Neoptolemus and Archelaus routed the Bithynian army on the river Amnias, and captured the camp and military chest. It was a fierce and for some time a doubtful fight, and seems to have been decided by the scythed chariots, which spread terror in the Bithynian ranks. [Victory over Aquillius.] Nicomedes fled to Aquillius, who was defeated by Archelaus near Mount Scorobas, and fled with the king across the Sangarius to Pergamus, whence he attempted to reach Rhodes. Cassius retreated to Phrygia, and tried to discipline his raw levies. But, finding this impossible; he broke up the army and led the Roman troops with him to Apameia. The fleet in the Black Sea was surrendered by its commander.

[Mithridates' progress through Phrygia, Mysia and Asia.] Thus, triumphant by sea and land, Mithridates, after settling Bithynia, marched through Phrygia and Mysia into the Roman province Asia, and was hailed everywhere as a deliverer, for after his victories he had sent home all his Asiatic prisoners with presents. Then he sent messengers into Lycia and Pamphylia to seek the alliance of those countries. Oppius was in Laodicea, on the Lycus. The king offered the townsmen immunity if they surrendered him, and, when they did so, carried him about as a show. [Fate of Aquillius.] Aquillius was also given up by the Mytileneans and made to ride in chains on an ass, calling out who he was wherever he went. At Pergamus Mithridates slew him by pouring molten gold down his throat—a savage punishment, which, however, confirms the impression that it was Roman avarice which forced on the war. Magnesia on the Maeander, Ephesus, and Mitylene welcomed the king joyfully, and Stratoniceia, in Caria, was captured. He then attacked Magnesia near Mount Sipylus, prepared to invade Rhodes, and issued a hideous order for an exterminating massacre of every Roman and Italian in Asia on an appointed day. Punishments were proclaimed for anyone who should hide one of the proscribed or bury his body; rewards were promised for all who killed or denounced them. Slaves who slew their masters were to be freed. The murder of a creditor was to be taken as payment by a debtor of half his debt. [Massacre of Romans and Italians.] There were dreadful scenes on the fatal day—the thirtieth after the order was issued—in the Asiatic cities. In Pergamus the victims fled to the temple of Aesculapius, and were shot down as they clung to the statues. At Ephesus they were dragged out from the temple of Artemis and slain. At Adramyttium they swam out to sea, but were brought back and killed, and their children were drowned. At Cos alone was any mercy shown. There those who had taken refuge in the temple of Aesculapius were spared. The number of the slain was said to be 80,000 or even 120,000, which must have been, however, an incredible exaggeration. [Objects of the massacre.] By this fiendish crime Mithridates must, though he was mistaken, have felt that he cut himself off for ever from all reconciliation with Rome. But no doubt he acted on calculation. For not only did he get rid of men who might have recruited the Roman armies; not only did he gratify the long-hoarded hatred of the farmers and peasants of whom Roman publicans and Roman slave-masters had so long made a prey; not only did he oblige the debtors by wiping out their debts and even the very memory of them in their creditors' blood, but he might well count on putting his accomplices also beyond the pale of Roman mercy, and so linking them to his own fortunes. Moreover, vengeance seemed remote. For Sulla had just marched on Rome instead of to the east, and a civil war in Italy might make Mithridates permanently supreme in Asia. [Mithridates' settlement of his new acquisitions.] So he made Pergamus his capital, leaving Sinope to his son as vice-regent, while Cappadocia, Phrygia, and Bithynia were turned into satrapies. All arrears of taxes were remitted; and so wealthy had his spoils made him that exemption for five years to come was promised to the towns that had obeyed his orders.

But the tide was already on the turn. In Paphlagonia there was still resistance. Archelaus was repulsed and wounded at Magnesia. Mithridates in person was forced to abandon the siege of Rhodes. His revenge was sated; he was tired of the hardships of a war which he meant his generals to conduct in future; and with a new wife he went back to Pergamus, to his rings, and his music, and debaucheries, at the very time that a shudder had gone through Italy at the tidings of the massacre, and when Sulla was on his way to avenge it.

* * * * *

CHAPTER XII.SULLA IN GREECE AND ASIA.

A citizen of Athens, named Aristion, whose mother was an Egyptian slave, and who was the son or adopted son of one Athenion, had been sent by the Athenians as ambassador to Mithridates. He had been a schoolmaster and teacher of rhetoric, and professed the philosophy of Epicurus. He gained the ear of Mithridates, and sent home flaming accounts of the king's power, and of his intention of restoring the democracy at Athens. The Athenians sent some ships of war to bring him home from Euboea, with a present of a silver-footed litter; and in this, clothed in purple, and with a fine ring on his finger, which he had got probably from his friend Mithridates, he came back to Athens with much parade. [Revolt of Athens from Rome.] In a set speech he dilated on the king's splendid successes, and advised the people to declare themselves independent and elect him their general. They did so, and he very soon massacred his opponents and made himself despot. Thus Athens and the Piraeus passed into the hands of Mithridates. The spirit of disaffection to Rome spread rapidly. [Revolt of the Achaeans, Laconians, and Boeotians.] When Archelaus appeared in Greece, the Achaeans, Laconians, and Boeotians, with the exception of Thespiae, joined him, while the Pontic fleet seized Euboea and Demetrias, a town at the head of the gulf of Pagasae.

Sura was sent by the Roman governor of Macedonia to make head against the invaders. He won a naval battle and captured Sciathus, where all the spoils of the enemy were stored. [Conflicts between the Romans and the forces of Mithridates in Boeotia.] Then he marched into Boeotia, and, after a three days' engagement with the combined forces of Archelaus and Aristion, pushed Archelaus back to the coast. The war, perhaps, might have been ended here; but at this moment Lucullus came to announce the approach of Sulla, and to warn Sura that the war had been entrusted to him. So Sura retired to Macedonia. [Sulla lands in Epirus, 87 B.C., and marches on Athens.] Sulla had left Brundusium in 87, and, landing on the coast of Epirus, gathered what supplies he could from Aetolia and Thessaly, and marched straight for Athens. It was soon seen that the foundations of the empire of Mithridates were based on sand. The Boeotians at once submitted, including Thebes, which had joined the king. [Siege of the Piraeus and Athens.] Sulla then began two sieges, that of the Piraeus where Archelaus was, and that of Athens defended by Aristion. Archelaus had before shown himself an intrepid soldier, and he baffled all Sulla's efforts with equal ingenuity and courage. After an unsuccessful attempt to storm the walls, Sulla retired to Eleusis and Megara, thus keeping up his communications with Thebes and the Peloponnese, and set to work constructing catapults and other engines, and preparing an earthwork from which he meant to attack the wall with them. For these purposes he cut down the trees of the Academia and the Lyceum. He was kept informed of intended sallies by two slaves inside the town, who threw out leaden balls with words cut on them. But as fast as the earthwork rose Archelaus built towers on the walls opposite to it, and thence harassed the besiegers. [Battle at the Piraeus. Archelaus nearly taken.] He was also reinforced by Mithridates, and then came out and fought a battle which was for some time doubtful; but he was forced to retire at length with the loss of 2,000 men. He himself remained till the last. The gates were shut and he had to be drawn up by a rope over the wall.

[Sulla's difficulties.] The affairs of Sulla, however, were in no flourishing condition. He had come to Greece with only 30,000 men, with no fleet, and little money. He was forced to plunder the shrines of Epidaurus, Olympia, and Delphi. His messenger to Delphi came back saying that he had heard the sound of a lute in the temple, and dared not commit the sacrilege. But Sulla sent him back, saying that he was sure the sound was a note of welcome, and that the god meant him to have the treasure. He promised to pay it back some day, and he kept his word, for he confiscated half the land of Thebes and applied the proceeds to reimbursing the sacred funds. In his worst straits he was always ready with some such mockery. [Sulla sends Lucullus to Egypt.] Winter was now at hand, and Sulla despatched Lucullus to Egypt to get ships. The refusal of the King of Egypt shows what was now thought of the Roman power. Sulla then formed a camp at Eleusis and continued the siege, and so shook the great tower of Archelaus by a simultaneous discharge of twelve leaden balls from his catapults that it had to be drawn back. [Blockade of Athens.] By means of the two slaves he was also able to frustrate the attempts of Archelaus to throw supplies into Athens, which was now suffering from hunger, for Sulla had surrounded it with forts and turned the siege into a blockade. Mithridates now sent his son into Macedonia with an army, before which the small Roman force there had to retire. After this success the prince marched towards Athens, but died on the way. [Desperate defence of the Piraeus.] At the Piraeus scenes occurred which were afterwards repeated at the siege of Jerusalem. Archelaus undermined the earthwork and Sulla made another determined attempt to take the wall by storm. He battered down part of it, fired the props of his mine and so brought down more, and sent troops by relays to escalade the breach. But Archelaus, like the Plataeans in the Peloponnesian war, built an inner crescent-shaped wall, from which he took the assailants in front and on both flanks when they tried to advance. [Sulla turns the siege into a blockade.] At last, wearied by this dogged resistance, Sulla turned the siege of the Piraeus also into a blockade, which meant simply that he hindered Archelaus from helping Athens, for he could not prevent the influx of supplies from the sea.

[Athens taken March 1, B.C. 86.] Athens meanwhile was in dreadful straits. Wheat was selling at nearly 3_l_. 10_s_. a gallon, and the inhabitants were feeding on old leather bottles, shoes, and the bodies of the dead. A deputation came out, but Sulla sent them back because they began an harangue on the deeds of their ancestors, put into their mouths, no doubt, by the rhetorician Aristion. Sulla told them they were the scum of nations, not descended from the old Athenians at all, and that instead of listening to their rhetoric he meant to punish their rebellion. On the night of March 1, 86 B.C., he broke into the town amid the blare of trumpets and the shouts of his troops. He told his men to give no quarter, and the blood, it was said, ran down through the gates into the suburbs. [Aristion slain.] Aristion fled to the Acropolis. Hunger forced him in the end to capitulate, and he was killed. Sulla meanwhile had forced on the siege of Piraeus still more vigorously. He got past the crescent wall, only to find other walls similarly constructed behind it; but he gradually drove Archelaus into Munychia, or the peninsular part of Piraeus, and as he had no ships he could do nothing more. [Archelaus sails from Piraeus, and joins Taxiles, sent by Mithridates with reinforcements.] Either before or after the capture of the Acropolis Archelaus sailed away, in obedience to a summons from Taxiles, a new general whom Mithridates had sent with an army of 100,000 foot, 10,000 horse, and ninety scythed chariots into Greece. With these forces and the troops previously sent with his master's son he formed a junction at Thermopylae, marched into Phocis down the valley of the Cephissus, attempted but failed to take Elateia, and came up with Sulla near Chaeroneia. [Sulla forms a junction with Hortensius.] Sulla had marched into Boeotia and joined Hortensius, who had a brought some troops from Thessaly. But he is said by Appian to have had not a third of the enemy's numbers, while Plutarch affirms that he had only 15,000 foot and 1,500 horse.

[Illustration: Map to illustrate the March of SULLA and ARCHELAUS before Chaeroneia.]

[Position of the two armies.] Sulla was on the west bank of the Cephissus, on an eminence named Philoboeotus, and Archelaus on the other side of the river not far off. Sulla's soldiers were alarmed by the numbers and splendour of the enemy, for the brass and steel of their armour 'kindled the air with an awful flame like that of lightning.' [Manoeuvres of Sulla and Archelaus.] Archelaus, marching down the valley of the Cephissus, tried to seize a strong position called the Acropolis of the Parapotamii, situated on the Assus, which joined the Cephissus to the south of both armies. But Sulla, who had wearied out his men by drudgery in dyke-making, and made them eager for a fight, crossed the Cephissus, seized the position first, and then, crossing the Assus, took up his position under Mount Edylium. Here he encamped opposite Archelaus, who, having also crossed the Assus, was now at a place called Assia, which was nearer Lake Copais. Thence Archelaus made an attempt on Chaeroneia; but Sulla was again beforehand with him, and garrisoned the place with one legion. South of Chaeroneia was a hill called Thurium. This Archelaus seized. Sulla then brought the rest of his troops across the Cephissus, to form a junction with the legion in Chaeroneia and dislodge the enemy from Thurium. He left Murena on the north of the Cephissus to keep the enemy in check at Assia. Archelaus, however, also brought his main army across the Cephissus after Sulla. Murena followed him, and Sulla drew up his army with his cavalry on each wing, himself commanding the right and Murena the left. The armies were now opposite each other, Sulla to the south, then Archelaus, then the Cephissus. [Battle of Chaeroneia.] Sulla sent some troops round Thurium to the hills behind Chaeroneia, and in the enemy's rear. The enemy ran down in confusion from Thurium, where they were met by Murena with Sulla's left wing, and were either destroyed or driven back upon the centre of the line of Archelaus, which they threw into disorder. Sulla on the right advanced so quickly as to prevent the scythed chariots from getting any impetus, by which they were rendered useless, for the soldiers easily eluded them when driven at a slow pace, and as soon as they had passed killed the horses and drivers. Archelaus now extended his right wing in order to surround Murena. Hortensius, whom Sulla had posted on some hills to the left of his left wing on purpose to defeat this manoeuvre, immediately pressed forward to attack this body on its left flank. But Archelaus drove him back with some cavalry, and nearly surrounded Hortensius.

[Illustration: First position of the two armies at CHAERONEIA.]

[Illustration: Second position of the two armies at CHAERONEIA.]

Sulla hastened to his aid, and Archelaus, seeing him coming, instantly counter-marched and attacked Sulla's right in his absence, while Taxiles assailed Murena on the left. But Sulla hastened back, too, after leaving Hortensius to support Murena, and, when he appeared, the right wing drove back Archelaus to the Cephissus. Murena was equally triumphant on the left wing, and the barbarians fled pell-mell to the Cephissus, only 10,000 of them reaching Chalcis in Euboea. [Sulla's falsehood about the battle.] Appian says the Romans lost only thirteen men, while Plutarch, on the authority of Sulla's Memoirs, says that they lost four. This is absurd. Sulla seems to have told some startling lies in his Memoirs, perhaps to prove that he had been the favourite of fortune, which was a mania of his.

[Dorylaus reinforces Archelaus.] Mithridates, when he heard of the defeat of Archelaus, sent Dorylaus with 8,000 men to Euboea, where he joined the remnant of the army of Archelaus, and crossing to the mainland met Sulla at Orchomenus. Sulla was in Phthiotis, to confront L. Valerius Flaccus who had come to supersede him, but he returned as soon as he heard that Dorylaus had landed. Orchomenus is just north of the Cephissus where it runs into Lake Copais, and a stream called Melas, rising on the east of Orchomenus, joined the Cephissus near its mouth, the neighbouring ground being a marsh. [Battle of Orchomenus. Disposition of Archelaus' army.] Archelaus did not want to fight, but Dorylaus hinted at treachery and had, no doubt, been ordered by Mithridates to avenge Chaeroneia. Near Mount Tilphossium, however, to the south of Lake Copais, he was worsted by Sulla in a skirmish, and thinking better of the advice of Archelaus tried to prolong the war. Archelaus, indeed, seems to have commanded in the battle, for Mithridates was shrewd enough to know when he had a good general. He drew up his army in four lines, the scythed chariots in front, behind them the Macedonian phalanx, then his auxiliaries, including Italian deserters, and, lastly, his light-armed troops. On each flank he posted his cavalry. [Sulla's arrangements.] Sulla, who was weak in cavalry, dug two ditches guarded by forts, one on each flank, so as to keep off the enemy's horse. Then he drew up his infantry in three lines, leaving gaps in them for the light troops and cavalry to come through from the rear when needed. To the second line stakes were given, with orders to plant them so as to form a palisade; and the first line, when the chariots charged, retired behind the palisade, while the light troops advanced through the gaps and hurled missiles at the horses and drivers. The chariots turned and threw the phalanx into confusion, and when Archelaus ordered up his cavalry, Sulla sent round his to take them in the rear. At one time, however, the contest was doubtful, and the Romans wavered, till they were put to shame by their general, who, seizing a standard and advancing towards the foe, cried out, 'When those at home ask where it was you abandoned your leader, say, it was at Orchomenus.' This great victory, in which Sulla showed generalship of a high order, ended the first Mithridatic war. The date is not quite certain.

Probably it happened in 86.

[Sulla winters in Thessaly.] After the battle Sulla wintered in Thessaly, where he built a fleet, being tired of waiting for Lucullus. [He confers with Archelaus at Delium.] At Delium he met Archelaus and each urged the other to turn traitor, Archelaus promising that Mithridates would aid Sulla against Cinna; Sulla advising Archelaus to dethrone Mithridates. It was a curious way of showing the respect which they entertained for each other's ability; but Sulla was too scornful of Asiatic aid, and Archelaus too loyal to listen to such suggestions. However, when Archelaus fell ill afterwards, Sulla was so attentive to him, besides giving him land in Euboea and styling him friend of the Roman people, that it was suspected that Archelaus had been playing into his hands all along. It was a most unlikely suspicion; for nothing was more natural than that now, when Sulla was making terms with Mithridates and going to meet Fimbria, he should wish to make Archelaus his friend. For after all he had resolved to forget the Asiatic massacre and not push Mithridates to desperation. [Terms offered by Sulla to Mithridates.] The terms agreed upon were these: Mithridates was to surrender Cappadocia, Paphlagonia, Bithynia, Asia, and the islands, eighty ships of war, all prisoners and deserters; he was to give pay and provisions to Sulla's men, and provide a war indemnity of 3,000 talents (732,000_l_.); to restore to their homes the refugees from Macedonia, and those whom, as will be related hereafter, he had carried off from Chios; and to hand over more of his ships of war to such states as Rhodes in alliance with Rome. Mithridates was then to be recognised as the ally of Rome. He chafed at the terms, the proposal of which indeed brought out the long-headed intrepidity of Sulla's character in the strongest light. Walking, as it were, on the razor-edge of two precipices, he never faltered once. The Romans could not charge him with not having carried into effect the original purpose of the war—the restoration of Nicomedes and Ariobarzanes—nor could Mithridates fail in the end to listen to the voice of Archelaus. When he at first rejected the terms, Sulla advanced towards Asia, plundering some of the barbarous tribes on the frontiers of Macedonia, and reducing that province to order. But Mithridates did not hesitate long. [Tyranny and difficulties of Mithridates.] He, too, was in a difficult position. The inhabitants of Asia Minor soon found that in yielding to him they had exchanged whips for scorpions. He suspected that the defeat of Archelaus at Chaeroneia would excite rebellion, and he seized as many of the Galatian chiefs as he could, and slew them with their wives and children. The consequence was that the surviving chiefs expelled the man whom he had sent as satrap. He suspected the Chians also, and made them give up their arms and the children of their chief men as hostages. Then he made a requisition on them for 2,000 talents (488,000_l_.), and because they could not raise the money, or because the tyrant pretended that there was a deficiency, the citizens were shipped off to the east of the Black Sea, and the island was occupied by colonists. The man who had managed the affair of Chios was sent to play the same game at Ephesus. But the people were on their guard, slew him, and raised the standard of rebellion. Tralles, Hypaepa, Metropolis, Sardis, Smyrna, and other towns followed their example. Mithridates tried to buoy up his sinking cause, attracting debtors by the remission of debts, resident aliens by the gift of the citizenship of the towns which they inhabited, and slaves by the promise of freedom—devices of a desperate man. A plot was laid against his life which was betrayed, and in his fury he launched out into yet more savage excesses. He sent a set of men to collect depositions, and they slew indiscriminately those who were denounced, 1600, it is said, in all.

[Fimbria mutinies against and murders Flaccus.] These events must have occurred in the winter of 86-85 B.C., when Flaccus was on his march from the Adriatic coast through Macedonia and Thrace for Asia. Flaccus had quarrelled with his lieutenant Fimbria, and superseded him. The

latter, when Flaccus had crossed from Byzantium to Chalcedon, induced the troops, who hated their general, to mutiny. Flaccus returned in haste; but, learning what had happened, fled back to Chalcedon and thence to Nicomedia. Here Fimbria, finding him hidden in a well, murdered him, and threw his head into the sea. [He defeats the son of Mithridates and pursues the king.] Then, attacking the king's son, he defeated him at the river Rhyndacus, and pursued the king himself to Pergamus and Pitane, where he would have taken him but that he crossed over to Mitylene, while Fimbria had no ships and was thus baulked of his prey. Another event had happened to aggravate his irritation. [Lucullus off the coast of Asia Minor. Overtures of Fimbria to him.] Lucullus, sent by Sulla to collect a fleet, had, as has been related (p. 153), failed in Egypt. But he had procured ships from Syria and Rhodes, induced Cos and Cnidus to revolt, and driven out the Pontic partisans from Chios and Colophon. He was now in the neighbourhood, when Mithridates was at Pitane. [Mithridates meets Sulla and thy come to terms.] But, he turned a deaf ear to Fimbria's request for aid, and after defeating Neoptolemus, the king's admiral, met Sulla in the Thracian Chersonese, and conveyed him across to Dardanus, in the Troad, where Mithridates came to meet him. Each had one feeling in common—dread lest the other should make terms with Fimbria; and the bargain was soon struck in spite of Sulla's soldiers, who were thus after all baulked of the long-looked-for Asiatic campaign and their desire to take revenge for the great massacre. But Sulla, as we have seen (p. 153), got some money to quiet them; and they were in his power in Asia almost as much as he had been in theirs at Rome. He at once led them against Fimbria, who was near Thyatira, in Lydia. [Fimbria's men desert to Sulla. Fimbria commits suicide.] He summoned that leader to hand over his army, and the soldiers began to desert to him. Fimbria tried to force them to swear obedience to him, and slew the first who refused. Then he sent a slave to assassinate Sulla; and the discovery of this attempt so maddened Sulla's soldiers that Fimbria dared not trust even Sulla's promised safe-conduct and slew himself. [Sulla's measures.] Sulla incorporated his troops with his own army, and proceeded to regulate the affairs of Asia. Those towns which had remained faithful to Rome or had sided with him were liberally rewarded. All slaves who refused to return to their masters were slain. The towns that resisted were punished and their walls destroyed. The ringleaders in the massacre were put to death. The taxpayers were forced to pay at once the previous five years' arrears and a fine of 20,000 talents (4,880,000_l_.), and Lucullus was left to collect it. In order to raise this sum the unhappy Asiatics were obliged to mortgage their public buildings to the Italian money-lenders; but Sulla got the whole of it, and scarcely was he gone when pirates, hounded on by Mithridates, came, like flocks of vultures, to devour what the eagles had left.
* * * * *

CHAPTER XIII.SULLA IN ITALY.

Leaving Murena in Asia with Fimbria's legions, Sulla, in 84 B.C., with his soldiers in good humour, and with full coffers, at last set out homewards. Three days after sailing from Ephesus he reached the Piraeus. Thence he wrote to the Senate in a different style from that in which he had communicated his victory over Fimbria, when he had not mentioned his own outlawry. He now recounted the Senate all that he had done, and contrasted it with what had been done to him at Rome, how his house had been destroyed, his friends murdered, and his wife and children forced to fly for their lives. He was on his way, he said, to punish his enemies and those who had wronged him. Other men, including the newly-enfranchised Italians, need be under no apprehension. We do not know much of what had been going on at Rome beyond what has been related in a previous chapter. Cinna and Carbo, the consuls, were making what preparations they could when the letter arrived. But it struck a cold chill of dread into many of the Senate, and Cinna and Carbo were told to desist for a time, while an embassy was sent to Sulla to try and arrange terms, and to ask, if he wished to be assured of his own safety, what were his demands. But when the ambassadors were gone, Cinna and Carbo proclaimed themselves consuls for 83, so that they might not have to come back to Rome to hold the elections; and Cinna was soon afterwards murdered at Ancona. The tribunes then compelled Carbo to come back and hold the elections in the regular manner; and Lucius Cornelius Scipio Asiaticus and Caius Norbanus were elected.

Meanwhile the ambassadors had found Sulla in Greece, and had received his answer. [Sulla's response to an embassy from Rome.] He said that he would never be reconciled to such criminals as his enemies, though the Romans might, if they chose; and that, as for his own safety, he had an army devoted to him, and should prefer to secure the safety of the Senate and his own adherents. He sent back with the ambassadors some friends to represent him before the Senate, and, embarking his army at the Piraeus, ordered it to go round the coast to Patrae in Achaia, and thence to the shores opposite Brundisium. He, himself, having a fit of gout, went to Euboea, to try the springs of Aedepsus. [Story of Sulla and some fishermen.] One day, says Plutarch, while he was walking on the shore there some fishermen brought him some fine fish. He was much pleased, but when they told him that they were citizens of Halae, a town which he had destroyed after the battle of Orchomenos, he said in his grim way, 'What! is there a man of Halae still alive?' But then he told the men to take heart, for the fish had pleaded eloquently for them. From Euboea he crossed to the mainland to rejoin his troops. They were about 40,000 in number, and more than 200,000 men were, he said, in arms against him in Italy. [Devotion of Sulla's troops to him.] But Sulla, who had connived at their mutinies, their vices, and their breaches of discipline, who had always led them to victory, and had never yet thrown aside that mask of moderation which veiled an inflexible determination to be revenged—Sulla who had been so long the sole representative of authority, and to whom they had learned to look for their ultimate reward, was their hero and hope. They offered him their money, and of their own accord swore not to disperse or to ravage the country. Sulla refused their money. Indeed he must have had plenty of his own. But now, when slowly and still very cautiously he was unfolding his designs, such devotion must have been very welcome.

[Sulla lands at Brundisium, B.C. 83.] Early in 83 he sailed from Dyrrhachium to Brundisium, and was at once received by the town. He was particularly anxious not to rouse against himself the Italians, with whom his name was anything but popular, and he solemnly swore to respect their lately-acquired rights. Adherents soon flocked to him. [He is joined by Crassus;] Marcus Licinius Crassus came from Africa, and was sent to raise troops among the Marsi. He asked for an escort, for he had to go through territory occupied by the enemy. 'I give thee,' said Sulla hotly, 'thy father, thy brother, thy friends and thy kinsmen, who were cut off by violence and lawlessness, and whose murderers I am now hunting down.' [by Metellus Pius;] Quintus Metellus Pius came from Liguria, whither he had escaped from Africa, after holding out there against the Marians as long as he could. [by Ofella;] Quintus Lucretius Ofella also came, soon to find to his cost that he had chosen a master who could as readily forget as accept timely service. [by Cn. Pompeius;] Most welcome of all was Cneius Pompeius, welcome not only for his talents, energy, and popularity, but because he did not come empty-handed. He had taken service under Cinna, but had been looked on with distrust, and an action had been brought against him to make him surrender plunder which his father, Cneius Pompeius Strabo, was said to have appropriated when he took Auximum. Carbo had pleaded for him, and he had been acquitted. But, as soon as Sulla was gaining ground in Italy, he went to Picenum where he had estates, and expelled from Auximum the adherents of Carbo, and then passing from town to town won them one by one from his late protector's interests, and got together a corps of three legions, with all the proper equipment and munitions of war. Three officers were sent against him at the head of three divisions; but they quarrelled, and Pompeius, who is said to have slain with his own hand the strongest horseman in the enemy's ranks, defeated one of them and effected a junction with Sulla somewhere in Apulia. Sulla's soldierly eye was pleased at the sight of troops thus successful, and in good martial trim; and when Pompeius addressed him as Imperator, he hailed him by the same title in return. Or, perhaps, he was only playing on the youth's vanity, for Pompeius, who was for his courage and good looks the darling of the soldiers and the women, was very vain, and flattery was a potion which it seems to have been one of Sulla's cynical maxims always to administer in strong doses. [by Philippus;] Later on he was joined by Philippus, the foe of Drusus, who for shifty and successful knavery seems to have been another Marcus Scaurus; [by Cethegus;] by Cethegus, who had been one of his bitterest enemies, which to a man of Sulla's business-like disposition would not be an objection, so long as he could make himself useful at the time; [by Verres.] and by Caius Verres, a late quaestor of Carbo, who had embezzled the public money in that capacity, and thus began by tergiversation and theft a notorious career.

Sulla marched northwards through Apulia, gaining friends by committing no devastation, and sending proposals of peace to the consul Norbanus, which were as hypocritical as was his abstinence from ravaging the country. He meant to deal with these Samnites through whose country he was marching at some other time. At present it was most politic not to provoke them. According to Appian, he met the consul at Canusium, on the Aufidus. [Battle of Mount Tifata. Defeat of Norbanus.] But it is probable that this is a mistake, and that the first battle was fought at Mount Tifata, a spur of the Apennines, near Capua. Norbanus had seized Sulla's envoys, and this so enraged the soldiers of the latter that they charged down the hill with irresistible impetuosity, and killed 6000 of the foe. Norbanus fled to Capua. Only seventy of the Sullans were killed. Sulla now crossed the Volturnus, and marching along the Appian Road met the other consul, Scipio, at Teanum, with whom he opened negotiations. Scipio sent Sertorius to Norbanus, who was blockaded in Capua, to consult him on the terms proposed. Sertorius, who had guessed what was coming and hoped to prevent it by something more efficacious than the advice of Norbanus, went out of his way and seized Suessa. This would interrupt Sulla's immediate communications with the sea, of which he was master. Sulla complained; but all the while he was, as Sertorius had warned Scipio, corrupting the Consul's troops. [Scipio's troops desert to Sulla.] They murmured when Scipio returned the hostages which Sulla had given; and, when the latter on their invitation approached their lines they went over to him in a body. On hearing of this Carbo said, that in contending with Sulla he had to contend with a lion and a fox, and that the fox gave him most trouble.

It may be noted here that Sulla, whose calculated moderation was paying him well—the more pleasantly because he knew that he could wreak his revenge afterwards at his leisure—never scrupled to employ every kind of subterfuge and lie. [Sulla's mendacity.] He tricked and lied on his march to Rome in 88. He lied foully to the Samnites after the battle of the Colline Gate. And he lied in his Memoirs, when he said that he only lost four at Chaeroneia, and twenty-three at Sacriportus, where he also said that he killed 20,000 of the foe. Absurd assertions like these may have been dictated as a sort of lavish acknowledgment paid to fortune, of whom he liked to be thought the favourite—lies that no one believed or was expected to believe, but keeping up a fiction of which it was his foible to be proud. [His success due greatly to desertions.] Another thing we may note is, that this was only the first of a long series of treasons to which, as much almost as to his own generalship, Sulla owed his final success. Five cohorts deserted at Sacriportus. Five more went over from Carbo to Metellus. Two hundred and seventy cavalry went over from Carbo to Sulla in Etruria. A whole legion, despatched by Carbo to relieve Praeneste, joined Pompeius. At the battle of Faventia 6000 deserted, and a Lucanian legion did the same directly afterwards. Naples and Narbo were both banded over by treachery. We hear also of commanders deserting. On the other hand, nothing is said of anyone deserting from Sulla, so that from the very beginning the contest could never have been really considered doubtful. [Sertorius sent to Spain. No capable man left to oppose Sulla.] After this signal success at Teanum Sertorius was sent to Spain, either because, as is likely, he made bitter comments on the consul's incompetence, or because it was important to hold Spain as a place for retreat. Carbo hastened to Rome to and at his instigation the Senate outlawed all the senators who had joined Sulla—a suicidal step, which would contrast fatally with Sulla's crafty moderation. [Burning of the Capitol.] It was about this time that the Capitol, and in it the Sibylline books, were burnt. Some people said that Carbo burnt it, though what his motive could be is difficult to conjecture. Sulla very likely regretted the loss of the Sibylline books as much as any man. [Sulla's situation at the close of 83 B.C.] With this the first year of the civil war ended. Sulla was master of Picenum, Apulia, and Campania; had disposed of two consuls and their armies; and had, by conciliation and swearing to respect their rights, made friends of some of the newly-enfranchised Italian towns.

The consuls for the next year (82) were Carbo and young Marius. The Marian governor in Africa was suspected of wishing to raise the slaves and to make himself absolute in the province. Consequently the Roman merchants stirred up a tumult, in which he was burnt alive in his house. In Sardinia the renegade Philippus did some service by defeating the Marian praetor, and so securing for Sulla the corn supply of the islands. In the spring Sulla seized Setia, a strong position on the west of the Volscian Mountains. Marius was in the same neighbourhood, and he retreated to Sacriportus on the east of the same range. [Battle of Sacriportus.] Sulla followed him, his aim being to get to Rome. A battle took place at Sacriportus. Marius was getting the worst of it on the left wing, when five cohorts and two companies of cavalry deserted him. The rest fled with great slaughter, and Sulla pressed so hard on them that the gates of Praeneste were shut, to hinder him getting in with the fugitives. Marius was thus left outside, and, like Archelaus at Piraeus, had to be hoisted over the walls by ropes. [Sulla wins the battle and besieges Praeneste.] Sulla captured 8000 Samnites in the battle, and now, for the first time, when the road to Rome was opened and victory seemed secure, showed himself in his true colours, and slew all of them to a man. [Massacre at Rome by order of young Marius.] An equally savage butchery had been going on in Rome, where Marius, before he was blockaded in Praeneste, had given orders to massacre the leaders of the opposite faction. The Senate was assembled as if to despatch business in the Curia Hostilia, and there Carbo's cousin and the father-in-law of Pompeius were assassinated. The wife of the latter killed herself on hearing the news. Quintus Mucius Scaevola, the chief pontiff, and the first jurist who attempted to systematise Roman law, fled to the temple of Vesta, and was there slain. The corpses of those who had been killed were thrown into the Tiber, and Marius had the ferocious satisfaction of feeling that his enemies would not be able to exult over his own imminent ruin. [Sulla comes to Rome.] Sulla, leaving Ofella to blockade Praeneste, hastened to Rome, but there was no one on whom to take vengeance, for his foes had fled. He confiscated their property, and tried to quiet apprehensions by telling the people that he would soon re-establish the State. But he could not stay long in the city, for matters looked threatening in the north.

[Metellus and Carbo in the north.] In this quarter the contest was more stubborn, because the newly enfranchised towns were stronger partisans of Marius. Metellus had fought a battle on the Aesis, the frontier river of Picenum, against Carrinas, one of Carbo's lieutenants, and after a hard fight had beaten him and occupied the adjacent country. This brought Carbo against him with a superior army, and Metellus could do nothing till the news of Sacriportus frightened Carbo into retreating to Ariminum, that he might secure his communications and get supplies from the rich valley of the Po. Metellus immediately resumed the offensive. He defeated in person one division of Carbo, five of whose cohorts deserted in the battle. His lieutenant, Pompeius, defeated Censorinus at Sena and sacked the town. Pompeius is also said to have crossed the Po and taken Mediolanum (Milan), where his soldiers massacred the senate. Metellus, meanwhile, had gone by sea along the east coast north of Ariminum, and had thus cut off Carbo's communications with the valley of the Po. This drove Carbo from his position, and he marched into Etruria, where he fought a battle near Clusium with Sulla, who had just arrived from Rome. In a cavalry fight near the Clanis, 270 of Carbo's Spanish horse went over to Sulla, and Carbo killed the rest. There was another fight at Saturnia, on the Albegna, and there, too, Sulla was victorious. [Indecisive combats.] He was less fortunate in a general engagement near Clusium, which after a whole day's fighting ended indecisively. Carbo was, however, now reduced to great straits. Carrinas was defeated by Pompeius and Crassus near Spoletum, and retired into the town. Carbo sent a detachment to his aid; but it was cut to pieces by an ambuscade laid by Sulla. Bad news, too, reached him from the south, where Marius was beginning to starve in Praeneste. [Carbo attempts to relieve Praeneste.] He sent a strong force of eight legions to raise the siege; but Pompeius waylaid and routed them, and surrounded their officer who had retreated to a hill. But the latter, leaving his fires alight, marched off by night, and returned to Carbo with only seven cohorts; for his troops had mutinied, one legion going off to Ariminum and many men dispersing to their homes. [A second attempt also fails.] A second attempt to relieve Praeneste was now made from the south. Lamponius from Lucania, whom we last heard of in the Social War (p. 120), and Pontius Telesinus from Samnium, marched at the head of 70,000 men into Latium. This movement drew Sulla from Etruria. He threw himself between Rome and the enemy, and occupied a gorge through which they had to pass before they could get to Praeneste. The Latin Road branches off near Anagnia, one route leading straight to Rome, the other making a detour through Praeneste. [The dead lock at Praeneste.] It was somewhere here that Sulla took his stand; and neither could the southern army break through his lines, nor Marius break through those of Ofella, though he made determined attempts to do so.

Meanwhile Carbo and Norbanus, released from the pressure of Sulla's army, struck across the Apennines to overwhelm Metellus; but their imprudence ruined them. [Overthrow of Carbo by Metellus.] Coming on Metellus at Faventia (Faenza) when their troops were weary after a day's march, they attacked him in the evening, hoping to surprise him. But the tired men were defeated. Ten thousand were killed; 6000 surrendered or deserted. The rest fled, and only 1000 effected an orderly retreat to Arretium. Nor did the disaster end here. A Lucanian legion, coming to join Carbo, deserted to Metellus on hearing the result of the battle, and the commander sent to offer his submission to Sulla. Sulla characteristically replied that he must earn his pardon, and the other, nothing loth, asked Norbanus and his officers to a banquet and murdered all who came. Norbanus refused the invitation and escaped to Rhodes; but when Sulla sent to demand that he should be given up he committed suicide. [Third attempt to relive Praeneste.] Carbo had still more than 30,000 men at Clusium, and he made a third attempt to relieve Praeneste by sending Damasippus with two legions to co-operate from the north with the Samnites on the south. [Carbo flies to Africa.] But Sulla found means to hold them in check, and Carbo, on the news of other disasters—at Fidentia, where Marcus Lucullus defeated one of his lieutenants, and at Tuder, which Marcus Crassus took and pillaged—lost heart and fled to Africa. Plutarch says that Lucullus, having less than a third of the numbers of the enemy, was in doubt whether to fight. But just then a gentle breeze blew the flowers from a neighbouring field, which fell on the shields and helmets of the soldiers in such a manner that they seemed to be crowned with garlands, and this so cheered them that they won an easy victory. After Carbo's flight his army was defeated by Pompeius near Clusium. [Carbo's lieutenants threaten Rome.] The rest of it, under Carrinas and Censorinus, joined Damasippus, and, taking up a position twelve miles from Rome in the Alban territory, threatened the capital and forced Sulla to break up his quarters, where he had been barring the roads to Praeneste and Rome. [Sulla comes to the rescue.] The sequel is uncertain; but it is probable that when the three commanders marched into Latium, Sulla was obliged to detach cavalry to harass them, and soon afterwards to march with all his forces to prevent Rome being taken. Why Carrinas did not assault Rome at once as he came south, we cannot say. Probably the relief of Praeneste was the most urgent necessity, and he hoped, after setting Marius free, to overwhelm Sulla first, then Pompeius, and then to take Rome. But, if these were his plans, the furious impetuosity of the Samnites disarranged them. [Desperate attempt of Pontius Telesinus.] Pontius, as soon as he saw Sulla's troops weakened, in order to oppose Carrinas, forced his way by night along the Latin Road, gathered up the troops of Carrinas on the march, and at daybreak was within a few miles of Rome. Sulla instantly followed, but by the Praenestine Road, which was somewhat longer; and when he got to Rome about midday, fighting had already taken place, and the Roman cavalry had been beaten under the walls of the city.

[Battle of the Colline Gate.] It was November, B.C. 82. Sunset was near and Sulla's men were weary, but he was determined or was compelled to fight. Giving his men some hasty refreshment, he at once formed the line of battle before the Colline Gate, and the last and most desperate conflict of the civil war began. Sulla's left wing was driven back to the city walls, and fugitives brought word to Ofella at Praeneste that the battle was lost. [Danger of Sulla.] Sulla himself was nearly slain. He was on a spirited white horse, cheering on his men. Two javelins were hurled at him at once. He did not see them, but his groom did, and he lashed Sulla's horse so as to make it leap forward, and the javelins grazed its tail. Sulla wore in his bosom a small golden image of Apollo, which he brought from Delphi. He now kissed it with devotion, and prayed aloud to the god not to allow him to fall ingloriously by the hands of his fellow-citizens, after leading him safe through so many perils to the threshold of the city. But neither courage nor superstition availed him against the fury of the Samnite onset. For the first time in his life Sulla was beaten, and either retreated into Rome or maintained a desperate struggle close to the walls during the night. On the right wing, however, Crassus had gained the day, had chased the foe to Antemnae, and halting there sent to Sulla for a supply of food. Thus apprised of his good fortune, he hastened to join Crassus. That division of the enemy which had beaten him had doubtless heard the same news, and must have dispersed or joined the rest of their forces at Antemnae. But in any case they were full of despair. Three thousand offered to surrender. But Sulla never gave mercy, though he often sold it for an explicit or tacit consideration. He swore to spare them if they turned on their own comrades. They did so, and Sulla, taking them to Rome with four or five thousand other prisoners, placed them in the Circus Flaminius and had them all slain.

[Sulla's cold-blooded ferocity.] He was haranguing the Senate in the temple of Bellona, and the cries of the poor wretches alarmed his audience; but he told them to attend to what he was saying, for the noise they heard was only made by some malefactors, whom he had ordered to be chastised. This last blind rush of the Sabellian bull on the lair of the wolves, which Pontius had told his followers they must destroy, had failed only by a hair's breadth, and since the days of the Gauls Rome had never been in such peril. But now at last Sulla had triumphed, and could afford to gratify his pent-up passion for vengeance. This butchery in the Circus was but the beginning of what he meant to do. [Executions.] The four leaders, Pontius, Carrinas, Damasippus, and Censorinus, were all beheaded; and, in the same ghastly fashion in which, it was said, Hannibal had learnt the death of Hasdrubal, so those blockaded in Praeneste learnt the fate of the relieving army and their own fate also by seeing four heads stuck on poles outside the town walls. They were half starving and could resist no longer. Marius and a younger brother of Pontius killed each other before the surrender. Ofella sent the head of Marius to Sulla, who had it fixed up before the Rostra, and jeered at it in his pitiless fashion, quoting from Aristophanes the line, You should have worked at the oar before trying to handle the helm.
[Massacre at Praeneste.] Then he went to Praeneste, and made all the inhabitants come outside and lay down their arms. The Roman senators who had been in the place had been already slain by Ofella. Three groups were made of the rest, consisting of Samnites, Romans, and Praenestines. The Romans, the women, and the children were spared. All the others, 12,000 in number, were massacred, and Praeneste was given over to pillage.
[Fate of Norba.] So ruthless an example provoked a desperate resistance at Norba. It was betrayed to Lepidus by night; but the citizens stabbed and hung themselves or each other, and some locking themselves inside their houses, set them in flames. A wind was blowing and the town was consumed. So at Norba there was neither pillage nor execution. Nola was not taken till two years afterwards, and we have seen (p. 121) what became of Mutilus on its surrender.
[Sulla's vengeance in Samnium.] Aesernia, the last Samnite capital in the Social War, was captured in the same year (80), and Sulla did his best to fulfil his threat of extirpating the Samnite name. In Etruria Populonium held out longer, and in Strabo's time was still deserted—a proof of the punishment which it received. Volaterrae was the last town to submit. In 79 its garrison surrendered, on condition of their lives being spared. But the soldiers of the besieging force raised a cry of treason and stoned their general, and a troop of cavalry sent from Rome cut the garrison to pieces.
[Fate of Carbo. Pompeius in Sicily.] In the provinces there was still much to be done. Pompeius was sent to Sicily, and on his arrival Perperna, the Marian governor, left the island. Carbo had come over from Africa to Cossura, and was taken and brought before Pompeius. Pompeius condemned the man who had once been his advocate, and sent his head to Sulla. It is said that Carbo met his death in a craven way, begging for a respite. Whether this is true or not, he seems to have been a selfish and incapable man. But if it be true that Pompeius, while he had Carbo's companions instantly slain, purposely spared Carbo himself in order to have the satisfaction of trying him, he was less to be envied than the man he tried. He divorced his wife at this time in order to marry Sulla's step-daughter, who was also divorced from her husband for the purpose. From Sicily Pompeius was sent to Africa, where Lucius Domitius Ahenobarbus was in arms. Crossing offer with 120 ships and 800 transports he landed some of his troops at Utica and some at Carthage.
[Decay of discipline in Roman armies.] The decay of discipline in the Roman armies is illustrated by an incident which occurred at Carthage. One soldier found some treasure, and the

rest would not stir for several days till they were convinced that there was nothing more to be found. Pompeius looked on and laughed at them. Sulla's way of treating his soldiers was already bearing fruit, and was one of the worst of the evils which he brought on Italy; for he who goes about scattering smiles and smooth words in order to win a name, for good-nature will always find others to run him a race in such meanness, and so discipline becomes subverted and states arc ruined.

[Domitius Ahenobarbus conquered and slain by Pompeius in Africa.] Pompeius found Domitius strongly posted behind a ravine. Taking advantage of a tempest, he crossed it and routed the enemy. His men hailed him Imperator: but he said he would not take the title till they had taken the camp. The camp was then stormed and Domitius slain. Pompeius also captured the towns held by the partisans of Domitius, and defeated and took prisoner the Marian usurper who had expelled Hiempsal, King of Numidia. Hiempsal was restored and his rival put to death. On returning to Utica Pompeius found a message from Sulla, telling him to disband his troops except one legion and wait till his successor came. [Vanity of Pompeius.] The men mutinied, for they liked Pompeius, and Sulla was told that Pompeius was in rebellion. He remarked that 'in his old age it was his fate to fight with boys'—a saying to which Pompeius's speech, 'that more men worshipped the rising than the setting sun,' may have been intended as a rejoinder. But soon he was relieved by hearing that the politic Pompeius had appeased the mutiny. Sulla had the art of yielding with a good grace when it was necessary, and, seeing how popular Pompeius was, he went out to meet him on his return and greeted him by the name 'Magnus.' The vain young man asked for a triumph. His forty days' campaign had indeed been brilliant; but he was not even a praetor, the lowest official to whom a triumph was granted, nor a senator, but only an eques. Sulla at first was astonished at the request, but contemptuously replied, 'Let him triumph; let him have his triumph.'

[Sulla has Ofella slain.] Two other officials of Sulla gave him trouble. One, Ofella, stood for the consulship against his wishes, and went about with a crowd of friends in the Forum. But with a man like Sulla it was foolish to presume on past services. He had no notion of allowing street-riots again, and sent a centurion who cut Ofella down. The people brought the centurion to him, demanding justice. [Sulla's parables.] Sulla told them the man had done what he ordered, and then spoke a grim parable to them. A rustic, he said, was so bitten by lice that twice he took off his coat and shook it. But as they went on biting him he burnt it. And so those who had twice been humbled had better not provoke him to use fire the third time. [Murena provokes the second Mithridatic war.] The other officer was Murena, who had been left in Asia. He raised troops besides the legions left with him, forced Miletus and other Asiatic towns to supply a fleet, and then stirred up the second Mithridatic war. The Colchians had revolted, and Mithridates suspected his son of fostering the revolt in order to be set over them. So he invited him to come to his court, put him there in chains of gold, and soon killed him. He had also, it seems, threatened Archelaus, who fled from him and represented to the ready ears of Murena, that Mithridates still held part of Cappadocia, and was collecting a powerful army. Murena advanced into Cappadocia, took Comana, and pillaged its temple. Mithridates appealed to the treaty; but Murena asked where it was, for the terms had never been reduced to a written form. [Mithridates appeals to the Senate.] The king then sent to the Senate. Murena crossed the Halys, and retired into Phrygia and Galatia with rich spoil. [Murena defeated.] Disregarding a prohibition of the Senate, he again attacked the king, who at last sent Gordius against him, and soon after, coming up in person, defeated Murena twice and drove him into Phrygia. For this success Mithridates lit on a high mountain a bonfire, which, it is said, was seen more than a hundred miles away by sailors in the Black Sea. [Sulla puts a stop to the war.] Sulla sent orders to Murena to fight nor more; and Mithridates, on condition of being reconciled to Ariobarzanes, was allowed to keep as much of Cappadocia as was in his possession. He gave a great banquet in honour of the occasion; and Murena went home, where he had a triumph. Sulla probably granted it to him after his defeats with more pleasure than he granted it to Pompeius for his victories.

[Sertorius in Spain.] The ablest of the Marian generals was, it has been seen, virtually unemployed in the Civil War. Sertorius, when sent to Spain, seized the passes of the Pyrenees. Sulla, in 81, sent against him, Q. Annius Luscus, who found one of the lieutenants of Sertorius so strongly posted that he could not get past him. However this lieutenant was assassinated by one of his own men, and his troops abandoned their position. [He flies to Mauretania. At Pityussa.] Sertorius had few men, and fled to New Carthage, and thence to Mauretania. Here he was attacked by the barbarians, and re-embarking, was on his way back to Spain, when he fell in with some Cilician pirates with whom he attacked Pityussa (Iviza) and expelled the Roman garrison. [At Gades.] Annius hastened to the rescue and worsted him in a fight, after which Sertorius sailed away through the Straits of Gibraltar to Gades (Cadiz). Here some sailors told him of two islands which the Spaniards believed to be the Islands of the Blest, with a pleasant climate and a fruitful soil. In these islands—probably Madeira—Sertorius wished to settle. [In Mauretania.] But, when his Cilician allies sailed to Mauretania to restore some prince to his throne, he went there too and fought on the other side. Sulla sent help to the prince, but Sertorius defeated the commander and was joined by the troops. [Invited to Spain.] Now, when once more at the head of a Roman army, he was invited to Spain by the Lusitani, who were preparing to revolt against Rome. With 2,600 Romans and 700 Africans he crossed the sea, gaining a victory over the Roman cruisers on his way, and set to work organizing and drilling the Lusitani in Roman fashion. [His white fawn.] One of them gave him a white fawn, and Sertorius declared that it had been given him by Diana. After this, when he obtained any secret intelligence he said that the fawn had told him, and brought it out crowned with flowers, if it was some officer's success of which he had heard. By such means, and by introducing a gay and martial uniform among his troops, he made his army both well-disciplined and devoted to him personally, and defeated one governor of Further Spain on the Baetis (Guadalquiver). [Defeats Metellus Pius.] Gaining afterwards a series of successes over Q. Metellus Pius, who had been sent against him, he was still in arms and master of a considerable part of Spain when Sulla died.

* * * * *

CHAPTER XIV.THE PERSONAL RULE AND DEATH OF SULLA.

Sulla was to all intents and purposes a king in Rome. He harangued the people on what he had achieved, and told them that if they were obedient he would make things better for them, but that he would not spare his enemies, and would punish everyone who had sided with them since Scipio violated his covenant. Then began a reign of terror. Not only did he kill his enemies, but gave over to his creatures men against whom he had no complaint to make. At last a young noble, Caius Metellus, asked him in the Senate, 'Tell us, Sulla, when there is to be an end of our calamities. We do not ask thee to spare those whom those hast marked out for punishment, but to relieve the suspense of those whom thou hast determined to save.' Sulla replied that he did not yet know. 'Then,' said Metellus, 'let us know whom thou intendest to destroy.' Sulla answered by issuing a first proscription list, including eighty names. People murmured at the illegality of this, and in two days, as if to rebuke their presumption, he issued a second of 220, and as many more the next day. Then he told the people from the rostrum that he had now proscribed all that he

remembered, and those whom he had forgotten must come into some future proscription. Such a speech would seem incredible if put into the mouth of any other character it history; but it is in keeping with Sulla's passionless and nonchalant brutality. The ashes of Marius he ordered to be dug up and scattered in the Anio, the only unpractical act we ever read of him committing. Death was ordained for every one who should harbour or save a proscribed person, even his own brother, son, or parent. But he who killed a proscribed man, even if it was a slave who slew his master or a son his father, was to receive two talents. Even the son and grandson of those proscribed were deprived of the privileges of citizenship, and their property was confiscated. Not only in Rome but in all the cities of Italy this went on. Lists were posted everywhere, and it was a common saying among the ruffianly executioners, 'His fine home was the death of such an one, his gardens of another, his hot baths of a third,' for they hunted down men for their wealth more than from revenge. [Story illustrative of the time.] One day a quiet citizen came into the Forum, and out of mere curiosity read the proscription list. To his horror he saw his own name. 'Wretch,' he cried, 'that I am, my Alban villa pursues me!' and he had not gone far when a ruffian came up and killed him. [Sulla and Julius Caesar.] The famous Julius Caesar was one of those in danger. He would not divorce his wife at the bidding of Sulla, who confiscated her property if not his as well, being so far merciful for some reason which we do not know. [Story of Roscius.] One case has been made memorable by the fact that Cicero was the counsel for one of the sufferers. Two men named Roscius procured the assassination of a third of the same name by Sulla's favourite freedman, Chrysogonus, who then got the name of Roscius put on the proscription list, and, seizing on his property, expelled the man's son from it. He having friends at Rome fled to them, and made the assassins fear that they might be compelled to disgorge. So they suddenly charged the son with having killed his father. The most frightful circumstance about the case is not the piteous injustice suffered by the son, but the abject way in which Cicero speaks of Sulla, comparing him to Jupiter who, despite his universal beneficence, sometimes permits destruction, not on purpose but because his sway is so world-wide, and scouting the idea of its being possible for him to share personally in such wrongs. It has been well said, 'We almost touch the tyrant with our finger.' Cicero soon afterwards left Rome, probably from fear of Sulla.
[Wholesale punishment of towns.] It is said that the names of 4,700 persons were entered on the public records as having fallen in the proscriptions, besides many more who were assassinated for private reasons. Whole towns were put up for auction, says one writer, such as Spoletum, Praeneste, Interamna, and Florentia. By this we may understand that they lost all their land, their privileges, and public buildings, perhaps even the houses themselves. Others, such as Volaterrae and Arretium, were deprived of all privileges except that of Commercium or the right of trade. [Sulla rewards his soldiers and establishes a permanent party.] Sulla's friends attended such auctions and made large fortunes. One of his centurions, named Luscius, bought an estate for 10,000,000 sesterces, or 88,540_l_. of our money. One of his freedmen bought for 20_l_. 12_s_. an estate worth 61,000_l_. Crassus, Verres, and Sulla's wife, Metella, became in this way infamously rich. In spite of such nominal prices, the sale of confiscated estates produced 350,000,000 sesterces, or nearly 3,000,000_l_. of our money. Sulla approved of such purchases, for they bound the buyers to his interests, and ensured their wishing to uphold his acts after his death. With the same view of creating a permanent Sullan party in Italy, and at the same time to fulfil his pledges to the soldiers, he allotted to them all public lands in Italy hitherto undistributed, and all confiscated land not otherwise disposed of. In this way he punished and rewarded at a stroke. No fewer than 120,000 allotments were made and twenty-three legions provided for. There was in it a plausible mimicry of the democratic scheme of colonies which

Sulla must have thoroughly enjoyed. Thus in Italy he provided a standing army to support his new constitution. [The Cornelii.] In Rome itself, by enfranchising 10,000 slaves whose owners had been slain, he formed a strong body of partisans ever ready to do his bidding; these were all named Cornelii. A man is known by his adherents, and the worst men were Sulla's protégés. [Catiline.] Catiline's name rose into notoriety amid these horrors. He was said not only to have murdered his own brother, but, to requite Sulla for legalising the murder by including this brother's name in the list of the proscribed, to have committed the most horrible act of the Civil War—the torture of Marcus Marius Gratidianus. This man, because he was cousin of Marius, was offered up as a victim to the manes of Catulus, of whom the elder Marius had said, 'He must die.' This poor wretch was scourged, had his limbs broken, his nose and hands cut off, and his eyes gouged out of their sockets. Finally his head was cut off, and Cicero's brother writes that Catiline carried it in his hands streaming with blood. But no one would attach much importance to what the Ciceros said of Catiline, and two circumstances combine to point to his innocence of such extreme enormities. One is that it was the son of Catulus who begged as a boon from Sulla the death of this Marius, and his name was very likely confused with Catiline's in the street rumours of the time; and the other and more direct piece of evidence is, that Catiline was tried in the year 64 for murders committed at this time, and was acquitted. It is a curious thing that the obloquy which has clung to Catiline's name on such dubious reports has never attached in the same measure to the undoubted horrors and abominations of Sulla's career.

Sulla, though he meant above all to have his own way, had no objection to use constitutional forms where they could be conveniently employed. He made the Senate pass a resolution approving his acts, and, as there were no consuls in 82, after the death of Marius and Carbo, he retired from Rome for a while and told the Senate to elect an Interrex, in conformity with the prescribed usage under such circumstances. Then he wrote to the Interrex and recommended that a Dictator should be appointed, not for a limited time, but till he had restored quiet in the Roman world, and, with a touch of that irony which he could not resist displaying in and out of season, went on to say that he thought himself the best man for the post. [Sulla's power.] Thus, in November 82, he was formally invested with despotic power over the lives and property of his fellow-citizens, could contract or extend the frontiers of the State, could change as he pleased the constitution of the Italian towns and the provinces, could legislate for the future, could nominate proconsuls and propraetors, and could retain his absolute power as long as he liked. He might have dispensed with consuls altogether. But he did not care to do this. The consuls whom he allowed to be elected for 81 were of course possessed of merely nominal power. Twenty-four lictors preceded him in the streets. He told the people to hail him as 'Felix,' declared that his least deliberate were his most successful actions, signed himself 'Epaphroditus' when he wrote to Greeks, named his son and daughter Faustus and Fausta, boasted that the gods held converse with him in dreams, and sent a golden crown and axe to the goddess whom he believed to be his patroness. Like Wallenstein, he mingled indifference to bloodshed with extreme superstition and boundless self-confidence. But, as the historian remarks, 'a man who is superstitious is capable of any crime, for he believes that his gods can be conciliated by prayers and presents. The greatest crimes have not been committed by men who have no religious belief.' No doubt to his mind there was a sort of judicial retribution in all this bloodshed; and, as he tried to make himself out the favourite of the gods, so by formally announcing the close of the proscription lists for June 1, 81 B.C., he spread some veil of legality over his shameless violence. [Peculiarly horrible nature of Sulla's acts.] There is something particularly revolting in the business-like and systematic way in which he went about his murderous work, appointing a fixed time for it to end, a fixed list of the victims; a fixed price to be paid per head, a fixed exemption for the murderers from his own law 'De Sicariis.' Modern idolaters of a policy of blood and iron may profane history by their glorification of human monsters; but no sophistry can blind an independent reader to the real nature of Sulla's character and acts. He organized murder, and filled Italy with idle soldiers instead of honest husbandmen. He did so in the interests of a class—a class whose incapacity for government he had discovered; and yet, knowing that his re-establishment of this class could only be temporary, he fortified it by every means in his power, and then, after a theatrical finale, returned to the gross debaucheries in which he revelled. Anything more selfish or cynical cannot be conceived, and those who call vile acts by their plain names will not feel inclined to become Sulla's apologists.

When he died he left behind him, it is said, what he may have meant as his epitaph, an inscription containing the purport of three lines in the 'Medea'—

Let no man deem me weak or womanly,
Or nerveless, but of quite another mood,
A scourge to foes, beneficent to friends.

Pompeius, the only man who had successfully bearded him, was the only friend not mentioned in his will. If anything could palliate his remorseless selfishness it is the candour with which he confessed it. He had made a vast private fortune out of his countrymen's misery. When he surrendered his dictatorship he offered a tenth of his property to Hercules, and gave a banquet to the people on so profuse a scale that great quantities of food were daily thrown into the Tiber. Some of the wine was forty years old, perhaps wine of that vintage which was gathered in when Caius Gracchus died. [He divorces Metella and marries again.] In the middle of the banquet his wife Metella sickened, and in order that, as Pontifex, he might prevent his home being polluted by death he divorced her, and removed her to another house while still alive. Soon afterwards he married another wife, who at a gladiatorial show came and plucked his sleeve, in order, as she said, to obtain some of his good fortune. [His abdication.] The rest of his life was spent, near Cumae, in hunting, writing his memoirs, amusing himself with actors, and practising all sorts of debauchery. Ten days before he died he settled the affairs of the people of Puteoli at their request, and was busy in collecting funds to restore the Capitol up to the last. [His death.] Some say he died of the disease which destroyed Herod. Some say that there is no such disease. Others say that he broke a blood-vessel when in a rage. He is described as having blue eyes, and a pale face so blotched over that it was likened to a mulberry sprinkled with meal.

[Rivalry of Lepidus and Pompeius.] His death, 78 B.C., was the signal for that break-up of his political institutions to which he had wilfully shut his eyes. The great men at Rome began to wrangle over his very body before it was cold. Lepidus, whom Pompeius, against Sulla's wishes, had helped to the consulship, opposed a public funeral. The other consul supported it. Sulla had with his usual shrewdness divined the character of Lepidus, and told Pompeius that he was only making a rival powerful. Pompeius opposed Lepidus now, for he knew that the partisans of Sulla would insist on doing honour to his memory. [Funeral of Sulla.] Appian describes the funeral at length. 'The body was borne on a litter, adorned with gold and other royal array, amid the flourish of trumpets, and with an escort of cavalry. After them followed a concourse of armed men, his old soldiers, who had thronged from all parts and fell in with the procession as each came up. Besides these there was as vast a crowd of other men as was ever seen at any funeral. In front were carried the axes and the other symbols of office which had belonged to him as dictator. But it was not till the procession reached Rome that the full splendour of the ceremonial was seen. More than 2,000 crowns of gold were borne in front, gifts from towns, from his old comrades in arms, and his personal friends. In every other respect, too, the pomp and circumstance of the funeral was past description. In awe of the veterans all the priests of all the sacred fraternities were there in full robes, with the Vestal Virgins, and all the senators, and all the magistrates, each in his garb of office. Next, in array that contrasted with theirs, came the knights of Rome in column; then all the men whom Sulla had commanded in his wars, and who had vied with each other in hastening there, carrying gilded standards and silver-plated shields. There was also a countless host of flute-players, making now most tender, now most wailing music. A cry of benediction, raised by the senators, was taken up by the knights and the soldiers, and re-echoed by the people, for some mourned his loss in reality, and others feared the soldiers and dreaded him in death as much as in life, the present scene recalling dreadful memories. That he had been a friend to his friends they could not but admit; but to the rest, even when dead, he was still terrible. The body was exhibited before the rostra, and the greatest orator of the time spoke the funeral oration; for Faustus, Sulla's son, was too young to do so. Then some strong senators took up the litter on their shoulders and bore it to the Campus Martius, where kings only were wont to be buried. There it was placed on the funeral pyre; and the knights and all the army circled round it in solemn procession. And that was Sulla's ending.'

To the student of history the story of such a funeral seems like the prostration of a nation of barbarians before the car of some demon-god. If the strong personality of the man—with all that dauntless bravery, that unerring sagacity, that trenchant tongue—still after two thousand years fascinates attention, if we are forced to own that for sheer power of will and intellect he stands in the very foremost rank of men, yet we feel also that in the case of such superhuman wickedness tyrannicide would, if it ever could, cease to be a crime.

* * * * *

CHAPTER XV.SULLA'S REACTIONARY MEASURES.

It is difficult to say about part of the legislation of this period whether it was directly due to Sulla or not, just as some of the changes in the army may or may not have been due to Marius, but were certainly made about his time. The method of gathering together all the changes made within certain dates, attributing them to one man, and basing an estimate of his character on them, has a simplicity about it which enables the writer to be graphic and spares the reader trouble, but is an unsatisfactory way of presenting history. Enough, however, is known of Sulla's own measures to make their general tendency perfectly plain. His main object was to restore the authority of the Senate, and to do more than restore it, to give it such power as might, if it was true to itself, secure it from mob-rule on the one hand and tyranny on the other. Though he foresaw that his efforts would be futile, he was none the less energetic in making them, and may reasonably have hoped that they would at all events last his time, and enable him to enjoy himself in Campania, undisturbed by another revolution. Our acquaintance with his laws is only second-hand, for none of them survive in their original form. They are known as Leges Corneliae, a term which, though applicable to some other laws, is usually applied to those of his making.

The Senate had originally been an advising council. Then it had acquired superior authority, and issued commands to the magistrates. It was placed by Sulla in a still higher position. To fill up its exhausted ranks he admitted to it 300 of the equestrian order; and, though it is not certain what its numbers were to be, it is probable that they were fixed at about 500. Then he provided for keeping the list full for the future. Hitherto a man had become a senator either at the censor's summons (of which he was practically certain if he had been tribune or quaestor), or, if he had been consul, praetor or aedile. Sulla made the quaestorship instead of the aedileship the regular stepping-stone, and increased the number of the quaestors to twenty. He also, in all probability, though it is not certain, took away from the censors their right of conferring or taking away senatorial rank. 'Once a senator, always a senator,' was therefore now the rule; and as the quaestors, who were the main source of supply, were nominated by the Comitia Tributa, the Senate became a more representative as well as a more permanent body than before, and independent of the magistrates.

Secondly, we have seen that Sulla had given to the Senate by law the power which it had previously exercised only by custom, of deliberating on a measure before it was submitted to the vote of the Comitia. This was one security against any measure being carried against its interests. Before this the practice had been either for the Senate through the tribunes to submit a measure to the vote, or for the tribunes to submit a measure of their own after obtaining the Senate's authority to do so. Saturninus, as we have seen, had overridden this custom, and the only way in which the Senate could maintain its old privileges would have been either by proclaiming a justitium, as it did on that occasion, or by picking out some technical informality in the passing of the plebiscitum, had not Sulla thus made its previous authorisation absolutely indispensable. The tribunes, being deprived of the power of proposing a measure at will to the Comitia Tributa, would also lose the power of prosecuting anyone before it, and probably lost the right of convening meetings in order to address the people. Sulla, too, provided that those who had been tribunes should be ineligible to other offices, and, though the right of veto seems to have been left to them, it is not clear that it was left without restrictions, while the abuse of it was made a heavily punishable offence. It is likely also that he made senators the only persons eligible to the tribunate. Positively, therefore, by making the Senate's previous consent to a law necessary, and negatively by these limitations of the prerogative of the tribunes, legislative power was placed wholly in the Senate's hands.

Thirdly, the balance in the Comitia themselves was so adjusted that the voting would be mostly in the Senate's interests. Something has already been said of Sulla's changes on this head, in reverting to the Servian mode of voting (p. 129). Some explanation of what this means may be given here. Sulla did not abolish the Comitia Tributa; but the measures just mentioned, as they left the practical power of legislation with the Senate, left the formal power with the Comitia Centuriata. We know the origin of the Comitia Centuriata. We do not know the origin of the Comitia Tributa. But we do know that by degrees the latter obtained legislative power co-ordinate with that of the former, and that the Plebiscitum became as binding on the nation as the Lex. There were in short two parallel bodies in which the people could make laws—ranged in the one by tribes, and voting on measures submitted to them by their tribunes; ranged in the other by centuries, and voting on measures submitted to them by the consul. But as the State became more and more democratic, the Comitia Tributa was more used than the Comitia Centuriata, in which legislation was gradually confined to special matters assigned to them by law or custom. Besides these functions the Comitia Tributa decided on war or peace, elected the tribunes, aediles, and lesser magistrates, and also usurped judicial power, arraigning magistrates for their conduct in office, &c. The functions of the Comitia Centuriata were, as we have, seen, also legislative. They elected to the higher magistracies and exercised jurisdiction in capital cases, a function which grew out of the Roman citizen's right to appeal. Each century had one vote; and as by the Servian arrangement the first class, though containing fewest voters, had nevertheless, owing to its highest assessment, most votes, it could by itself outvote the other classes. At some time or other this classification was altered; and a new system, based partly on centuries and partly on tribes, came into use. Each tribe was divided into ten centuries, five of seniors and five of juniors. The first class consisted of one of each of these from each tribe, so that, as there were thirty-five tribes, each class would consist of seventy centuries. It is said by some that the first class included also thirty-five centuries, or eighteen centuries of equites. If this be true, the first class would still have retained the preponderance of votes. In any case it had the best of the voting, for even if it was decided by lot which century of all the centuries should vote first, still the first class voted second, and the moral effect of the wealthier and weightier citizens voting one way or other would naturally influence the votes of the other centuries. Moreover some say that the lot was confined to the centuries of the first class. Such then was the original and such the modified constitution of the Comitia Centuriata. [Sulla's legislation about the Comitia.] Appian expressly states that Sulla reverted to the original mode of voting. But he may be confusing things, and only mean that Sulla took the voting power from the Comitia Tributa and vested it in the Comitia Centuriata. And this probably is what Sulla did.

[Curtailment of the power of the consuls and praetors.] Fourthly, as Sulla weakened the censorship in order to exalt the Senate's authority at its expense, so, to prevent any individual again obtaining undue influence, he ordained that no man should be consul till he had been first quaestor and then praetor, and that no man should be re-eligible to a curule office till after an interval of ten years. This, however, was not enough. It was his object to curtail the powers of every magistrate. And therefore, though the consulate was not dangerous to the Senate in the sense that the tribunate was, he laid hands both on it and on the praetorship. [Previous powers of the two offices.] The functions of the consuls and praetors had hitherto been these. The consuls had the general superintendence of all except judicial matters at home, and the military superintendence in all the provinces except Sicily, Sardinia, and the two Spains, in which they only occasionally exercised their imperium. One praetor, the Praetor Urbanus, presided over civil suits between Roman citizens. Another, the Praetor Peregrinus, superintended such suits between a citizen and an alien or between two aliens. The other four were over the four above-mentioned provinces. In case of need one man could do the work both of the Praetor Urbanus and the Praetor Peregrinus, leaving his colleague free for a military command. Or the consul or praetor might have his term of office extended, being bound to continue in his command till a successor arrived. Or one consul might manage the ordinary functions of both, and the other be similarly left free for some special employment. The Senate could in any given year assign, as business to be superintended by a consul or a praetor, some military command or judicial commission, and then the consuls or praetors had to settle by lot or by agreement who should undertake it. As the State grew greater these special assignations had to be made oftener. [The new scheme.] There had been eight officials for eight offices; now five new superintendents had to be provided for Asia, Africa, Macedonia, Narbo, and Cilicia, as well as one for the Quaestio de Repetundis. To enable eight men to do the work of fourteen the Senate made prolongation of office for a second year the rule, and the officials confined by the nature of these duties to the city during these years of office were generally sent at the end of it to the transmarine provinces where most money was to be made. Sulla increased the six praetors to eight, and made the two years' term of office the legal term. But if this added to their power in appearance, he diminished it in reality by separating the civil from the military functions altogether. The consuls and praetors were to manage the civil business of Rome. The proconsuls and propraetors were to command the army. In the first year of office the two consuls had the general administration of Rome, and two of the praetors its judicial administration. The other six presided over the various courts. In the second the ten exercised the imperium in Sicily, Sardinia, the two Spains, Asia, Africa, Macedonia,

Cilicia, and the two Gauls, and none of them might stay in his province beyond thirty days after his successor's arrival; or, under penalties for treason, might leave his province during his term; or attack a foreign power without express leave from home. [Effect of the new scheme.] The effect of all this is plain. Whereas formerly the magistrates, directly elected in the Comitia, might combine civil and military authority, now the military authority could only be held by those whose term of office was prolonged by the Senate's pleasure; for, though the practice became invariable, it remained at the Senate's discretion to break through it when it chose.

[Co-optation restored to the colleges.] Fifthly, having thus lessened the power of the censors, consuls, praetors, and tribunes, he by way of compensation—a serio-comic compensation it must have seemed to his shrewd yet superstitious mind—restored the right of co-optation to the sacred colleges of augurs and pontiffs, and increased their numbers, thus multiplying harmless objects of rivalry analogous to the ribands and garters of modern courts.

Sixthly, he took away from the equites and restored to the Senate the judicia.

[Restoration of the Judicia to the Senate.] The judicia have been often mentioned, and something maybe said about them here. In civil suits the praetor, as we have seen, had the superintendence. Sometimes he decided a case at once. Sometimes, if he thought the case should be tried, he appointed a judex, giving him certain instructions by which after the investigation he must decide the case. His action here would be something like one of our judge's charges, but given before hearing the evidence. There is nothing to prove that a judex of this kind was at this time taken from any special class, or that Sulla interfered with the established mode of procedure. [Organisation of criminal courts.] It was about the constitution of the criminal courts that the long struggle had raged between the Senate and equites and here he made great changes. He found some permanent criminal courts (e.g. the Quaestio de Repetundis, or court for investigating cases of extortion in the provinces) already in existence. He instituted or settled others; but it cannot be ascertained how many of the following, which were in existence after his time, were due to him. There were at least nine of these permanent courts (Quaestiones Perpetuae): the Quaestio Majestatis; de vi; de sicariis &c; de veneficiis; de parricidio; de falso; de repetundis; peculatus; ambitus; or courts for trying cases of treason, violence, assassination, poisoning, parricide, forgery, extortion, embezzlement, and bribery. And there may have been more, e.g. de adulteriis and de plagiis, for trying cases of adultery and the enslavement of freemen. [Procedure in the courts.] His object in consolidating them was to take from the Comitia the settlement of criminal cases, and to obviate the necessity for appointing special commissions. For there was no appeal from the quaestio, and a special commission was seldom requisite when so many courts were available.

To preside in these courts there were six praetors; but, as there were more courts than praetors, a senator, called judex quaestionis, was appointed annually for each court where a president was wanting, something after the fashion by which one of our judges sometimes in press of business appoints a barrister as his deputy to clear off the cases. The praetor, or judex quaestionis, presided over the judices in each court, and the judices returned a verdict by a majority of votes, sometimes given by ballot, sometimes openly. In choosing these judices this was the process. The whole number available was, it is said, 300, divided into three decuriae. In any given case the praetor named the decuria from which the jurymen were to be taken, and then drew from an urn containing their names the number assigned by law for the case to be decided. Each side could then challenge a certain number, and fresh names were drawn from the urn in place of those challenged. What Sulla did was to supply these decuriae from the senators instead of the equites.

One of the permanent courts found by Sulla already existing was that of the Centumviri, who had jurisdiction over disputed inheritances. The members of it were elected by the tribes, three by each tribe, 105 in all. Though it was directly elected by the people, Sulla could apprehend no danger from such a court, and did not meddle with it.

[Other measures attributed to Sulla.] Other measures are attributed to Sulla on evidence more or less probable, such as the suppression of gratuitous distributions of corn; the abolition of the right of freedmen to vote, and of the reserved seats appropriated to the equites at public festivals; the re-establishment in Asia of fixed taxes instead of the farming system; the extension of Italy proper from the Aesis to the Rubicon, and the conversion of Cisalpine Gaul into a province. It may be considered certain that he did all that he could to humiliate the equites; but the settlement of Italy was probably not due to him.

[His minor measures.] Other minor laws of which he was the author dealt with specific criminal offences or social matters. One, as we have seen (p. 196) specified the penalties for all sorts of assassination and poisoning. Another dealt with forgery, another with violence to the person or property, another with marriage and probably adultery. Another was a sumptuary law, which is said to have limited the price of certain luxuries. If this was the case it was even sillier than other sumptuary laws, for it would have encouraged instead of checking gluttony. Lastly, there was a law for the settlement of his colonies through Italy, and at Aleria in Corsica.

[Effects of Sulla's legislation.] Sulla had for the moment undone by his legislation the work of ages. He gagged free speech by the disabilities attached to the tribunate. He kept the government within a close circle by his process of recruiting the Senate. He made the magistrates subordinate to the Senate. He filled Italy and Rome with his own partisans, and therefore with those of the Senate, and he gave back to the Senate that coveted possession of the judicia for which it had struggled so long with the equites. But a system which could endure only by the repression not only of hostile interests but of the ambition of its own adherents carried in itself the seeds of early dissolution. Almost before the reaction was complete a counter-reaction had begun. Abdication only revealed monarchy, and the broad road which Sulla had laid over the breakers and quicksands of revolution in reality paved the way to a throne.

[Sulla's abdication a farce.] When be abdicated, he offered to render account to anyone for his acts, and there is a story that one young man thereupon followed him to his home loading him with abuse, which Sulla listened to with meekness. If the story be true, the incident was probably a pre-arranged part of the ceremony of abdication, which in everything, except the fact that Sulla slipped off the cares of government, was of course a farce. His funeral showed what his real power continued to be, and, if another anecdote be true, just before his death he had a magistrate of Puteoli strangled because he had not collected in time his town's subscription to the restoration of the Capitol. He had in fact done mischievously what the Gracchi would have done beneficently; and greedy swordsmen occupied the soil which the tribunes would have divided peaceably among peaceable men. [The policy of the Gracchi justified by after events.] The civil wars and the triumvirates are the best vindication of the policy of the Gracchi, unless we can bring ourselves to fancy that the Gracchi created, instead of attempting wisely to satisfy, the demands of the age. By an orderly intermixture of Italians and foreigners with the corrupt body of Roman citizens new life might have been infused into the old system, and something foreshadowing modern representative government have been established, without proscription or praetorian rule. As it was, the vices of society only became aggravated at an era of violence, and the sharpest remedies failed to stay the creeping paralysis by which it was assailed.

The gradual depopulation of Italy has already been described. In spite of Sulla's colonies the ruin of the country must have been vastly accelerated by his civil wars and those which followed them. And, while the honest country class was dying out, the town class was ever plunging deeper into frivolity and voluptuousness. To defray the cost of the sumptuous life of the capital the fashionable spendthrift was forced to resort to extortion in the provinces, which, as we have seen, became so crying an evil that a permanent court existed for dealing with it before the time of Sulla. The greedy throve on usury, or involved the State in war, to fill their own purses. The fortunes amassed by an Aquillius, a Verres, a Lucullus, spoke as eloquently of Rome's rapacity abroad as did those of Crassus or Sulla in Italy. Such being the state of things under the government which Sulla strove to perpetuate, his character as a statesman deserves as strong reprobation as his conduct as a man. To lay down power from a sense of duty is one thing. Cynically to shrink from responsibility is another. The misery of the following half-century must be laid chiefly at Sulla's door. The inevitable goal to which everything was tending was as patent in his time as in the time of Augustus. Whatever may have been for the interest of the Roman aristocracy, monarchy was by this time for the interest of the Roman world.

LIST OF PHRASES

It has been suggested that the following List of Phrases occurring in the History may be useful. But the definitions are only approximately precise.

Aerarium. The State treasury.

Capite Censi. Roman citizens rated by the head only, as having no property.

Cives Romani. Citizens of Rome, a Roman colony, or a Municipium.

Clientes. Dependents of the Patres. Free, but not Cives Romani.

Comitia Centuriata. The subdivisions (193 or 194 in number) of the six classes into which the Romans were divided, according to property, were called Centuries, and the assembly of them Comitia Centuriata.

Comitia Tributa. The assembly in which the people voted according to the tribes or territorial divisions.

Dominium. Ownership.

Equites. Originally the men rich enough to maintain war-horses; afterwards the rich class corresponding to our city men.

Flamen. A priest of some particular god.

Frumentaria. Lex. A law for cheapening corn.

Imperator. The title given on the battle-field to a successful general by his soldiers.

Imperium. The power given by the State to an individual who was to command an army.

Interrex. An official appointed to hold an election of consuls when the regular mode of election had not been followed.

Judicia. Bodies of jurymen (judices) who tried criminal cases.

Jugerum. A measure of surface 240 feet long, 120 broad.

Justitium. A suspension of public business for some religious observance.

Latifundia. Large estates cultivated by slave-labour.

Latini. See p. 16.

Legati. Officers of the general's suite corresponding to our generals of division.

Libertini. The class of freedmen known as Liberti, with reference to freeborn men, Libertini with reference to each other.

Municipia. Conquered Italian towns having the right of acquiring property in the Roman State (Commercium), and marrying the daughter of a Roman citizen (Connubium), but unable to acquire the honours of the State (Jus Honoris), or to vote at Rome (Jus Suffragii).

Negotiatores. Money-lenders.

Nobiles. The offspring of men who had held a curule office.

Optimates. The senatorial party at and after the era of the Gracchi.

Patres. 1. Originally Cives Romani, the governing body at Rome. 2. Afterwards the Senate.

Patronus. A Pater with reference to a Client. A Dominus with reference to a Libertus.

Perduellio. Abuse of official position injurious to the State.

Pilum. A wooden shaft 4 feet long, with an iron head 2 feet 3 inches long. There was also a lighter kind.

Plebiscitum. 1. A resolution of the people. 2. Equivalent to lex.

Plebs. Originally the free citizens of Rome who had no political privileges.

Populares. The anti-senatorial party at and after the time of the Gracchi.

Possessor. An occupier of public land.

Praefectura. A Roman colony, or Municipium, in which a Roman Praefectus administered justice.

Proletarii. Roman citizens rated at less than 1,500 asses.

Publicani. Farmers of the revenue.

Rostra. A name given to the stage in the Forum where speakers addressed the people. So called because ornamented with beaks of ships captured from the enemy.

Scriptura. A tax paid to the State on cattle grazing on public land.

Socii. Free inhabitants of Italy. See p. 16.

Vectigal. 1. A tax of 1/10th of the year's crops. 2. The revenue produced by the Scriptura.

CPSIA information can be obtained at www.ICGtesting.com
Printed in the USA
LVOW10s0107020415

432910LV00019B/540/P